CORRUPT
AND
DEMOCRACY
IN
THAILAND

Pasuk Phongpaichit
Sungsidh Piriyarangsan

SILKWORM BOOKS

First published in 1994 by The Political Economy Centre, Faculty of Economics, Chulalongkorn University.

ISBN 974-7100-31-2

This edition published in 1996, reprinted in 1997, 1998, 1999 by Silkworm Books
54/1 Sridonchai Road, Chiang Mai 50100, Thailand.
E-mail: silkworm@pobox.com

Set in: Palatino 10 pt
Printed by O.S. Printing House, Bangkok

CONTENTS

PREFACE
TO THE SECOND EDITION

'The budget is like a popsicle that's passed around. Everyone gets a lick at it when it comes their way, so that by the time the one at the end of the line gets it, there's little left... Most of the time corrupt politicians and officials escape punishment. In fact, most of them continue to prosper and command respect in society.' [Nation 19/5/96]

There are two things remarkable about this quotation. First, the author was not an academic researcher, nor even an opposition politician. Rather he was Boon-ua Prasertsuwan, the Speaker of the Parliament and Deputy Leader of the ruling Chart Thai Party. Second, his estimate that as much as 50 per cent of budget project funds was 'licked' away in this fashion excited almost no attention. It rated a few column inches in a couple of newspapers, and brought forth no denials, no counter-claims, no denunciations, no anger.

Over the two years since this work was first published, the wave of anti-corruption sentiment has swept across Asia. It is hard to name a sizeable Asian country which has not been rocked by a major corruption scandal involving officials or politicians. Most observers agree that two main historical developments prepared the way for this wave. First, since the end of the Cold War those in power have not been able to brand any opposition, including liberal criticism of the abuse of power, as a communist threat to the political order. Second, members of the growing middle class have made an issue of corruption, partly because they dislike seeing their own tax payments being hijacked, partly because they believe corruption gets in the way of economic and social progress.

Among all the Asian scandals, the two most important have occurred in India and South Korea.

In India, corruption had long seemed to be an intrinsic and unremarkable element of the political system. Yet in the mid-1990s, revelations of political corruption have contributed to a political revolution. First, the ruling Congress Party was beset by a string of allegations over kickbacks from foreign firms, particularly firms selling arms and other expensive high-technology equipment. Second, the prosecution of a large-scale financial hustler uncovered that he was systematically corrupting many politicians and officials on behalf of a wide variety of lobby clients. Rocked by these two scandals, the Congress Party which had dominated Indian politics for the half-century since independence, was forced into elections, decimated at the polls, and pushed onto the opposition benches.

In South Korea, allegations of corruption contributed to the fall of the old military-backed dictatorship, and the institution of an elected presidency. Even more remarkably, the elected president then proceeded to arrest two past military presidents along with some associates, and put them on trial for corruption and the abuse of power. At the end of the trial one ex-president was sentenced to death, the other to a long prison term, both were fined heavily for corruption, and seven of Korea's top corporate leaders were found guilty of corrupting them.

Often in the past, corruption scandals have focused on the small players. A few minor participants could be sacrificed for the sake of appearances, while the major players remained beyond reach. In India and Korea, the scandals have involved huge amounts of money, and have gone right to the top of the political tree. India's Congress Party government crumbled after seven ministers had been prosecuted, and the prime minister had been seriously implicated. In Korea, a leading politician commented: 'Never in Korean history has a King imprisoned two former Kings.'

Through these and other recent Asian corruption cases, there have been three recurrent themes in the way these scandals were unearthed and elevated into major political events.

First, the press has played a leading role in making these scandals into public causes. In India, a single TV journalist brought the huge lobbying scandal to public attention, after official investigators had twice brushed it under the carpet. Second, new-generation politicians, often lawyers or other professionals, have spear-headed the corruption charges, and fought off attempts to have them suppressed. The prime example is Korea's reforming president, Kim Young Sam. Third, the judiciary has played a crucial part in converting corruption charges into criminal convictions. In India, the high court took up the lobbying case after the politicians had attempted to suppress it. In Korea, a change in the law made it possible for the judiciary to take an active role in pursuing corruption by investigating bank accounts.

To what extent are these themes reflected in Thailand? First, the press is playing an important and growing role in investigating and exposing examples of political corruption. Indeed, as authors of this book, we have been surprised at the sustained press interests in its contents, which has led eventually to this reprinting. Second, parliament is slowly realising its role in checking the abuse of power by officials and politicians. In the no-confidence debate of May 1996, the opposition demonstrated a new level of research into political malpractice, particularly over the Bangkok Bank of Commerce. Third, the judiciary has begun to show signs of independent assertiveness, for instance over the Buriram vote buying case.

But we still have a long way to go. Thai officials and politicians still believe that the Korean and Indian examples could not be reproduced in Thailand. During the Banharn government, the term 'money politics' has come into general use. The cabinet has been jokingly compared to a convenience store, 'open 24 hours'. As this edition goes to press, one ex-minister is in court for vote-buying; another is charged with manipulation of land deeds, and suspected of share-market manipulation; the prime minister's family is under investigation for a corrupt land deal; and one deputy prime minister who resigned his post promptly presented another political figure with an 8 million baht Daimler as thanks for assistance in business.

For this reprint, we have made some small sub-editing changes to the original text, but we have not changed any of the facts, arguments or opinions. The problems remain the same. The solutions, we believe, must be based on popular pressure.

Pasuk Phongpaichit
Sungsidh Piriyarangsan

September 1996

PREFACE
TO THE FIRST EDITION

When this project began in June 1991, no one in the research team could anticipate the extent to which corruption would become a major political issue in many countries across the world.

The main focus was Italy. In 1992 a Milano businessman who had a contract to clean a municipal nursing home complained that he was being forced to pay a 10 per cent kickback to the politician who ran the home. The Milan magistrate took up the case. The accused politician was found guilty. Suddenly thousands of similar complaints were filed and the magistrates launched 'Operation Clean Hands'. The subsequent investigations extended through the local government network, to the central bureaucracy, to every political party, and to the major business corporations. Some 40,000 government officials may have been involved in all kinds of corruption, and in all 200,000 bureaucrats, businessmen, and politicians were subject to charges. It was estimated that in 1991 alone up to 15 per cent of the nation's US $100 billion budget deficit was accounted for in kickback money. A top state administrator shot himself to evade investigation. An ex-prime minister was accused of masterminding the murder of an ex-president. The scandals led to a popular demand for large-scale reform of the political system. The political parties which had dominated the parliament for over a generation disintegrated.

The movement was not confined to Italy. In Russia the government led by Yeltsin faced many problems of corruption charges. In China scandalous corruption in the Central Bank weakened the government's political stability. In India the prime minister was charged with accepting commission fees from arms purchases and becoming involved in shady deals in the stock market. In South Korea, a civilian candidate used corruption issues to raise support to oust the long-standing military-dominated government. In the United Kingdom several ministers had to resign on charges of corrupt involvement with business interests.

In Japan, a long string of corruption scandals finally brought down the Liberal Democrat Party which had dominated Japanese politics since the second world war. In Germany, the Christian Democrat Party lost public standing as a result of corruption scandals. In France, Mitterand's Socialist Party also lost popularity and electoral support in part as a result of corruption scandals.

In some of the world's poorer countries, corruption was blamed for the consistent failure to promote economic development. In the 1960s, Nigeria had been expected to emerge as one of the more successful developing countries on account of its rich oil resources, large population base, and good basic infrastructure. Post mortems in the 1980s concluded that the military rulers had consistently skimmed off the economic surplus through systematic corruption, resulting in low growth, persistent poverty, food shortages, and warlord politics. While Nigeria was the world's tenth largest petrol producer, Nigerians had to queue at the petrol pumps and pay a bribe to get a full tank. Eliminating such deep-rooted and systematic corruption is likely to require time and involve violence.

In Thailand, the military used the corruption of the Chatichai government as a major justification for the coup in February 1991. By 1992, however, many people had begun to see the dangers of corruption under a dictatorial or semi-dictatorial regime. Many businessmen, in particular, were keen to support this project and survey.

The results of this study were first revealed through a seminar held in June 1993. The findings received wide publicity in the local media. General Pramarn Adireksarn, the leader of Chart Thai, the major opposition party in parliament, threatened to sue the authors for libel. This threat redoubled the publicity, and helped to fuel a wider public debate on the issue of corruption in the Thai political system. The public debate enabled many people to understand why corruption is an issue which can change politics, to question how it may be controlled, and to reconsider what standards ought to be demanded from politicians and public officials. It is hoped these debates have made some contribution to strengthening civilian rule, and developing the necessary popular foundations for a stronger democracy and a better society.

This study could not have been completed without the encouragement, support, participation, and advice of many people and institutions.

Colleagues at the Faculty of Economics, Chulalongkorn University have helped in many ways. We would like to acknowledge in particular the assistance of the Dean, Professor Thienchay Kirananda; Assistant Professors Chatthip Nartsupha, Chomploen Chandraruangphen, Sriwong Sumitr, Somphop Manarangsan, Kanoksakdi Kaewthep, Samart Chiasakul, Sumalee Pitayanond, Ratana Sayakhanit; Associate Professors Narong Petchprasert, Kitti Limskul, Nualnoi Treerat and Acharn Duangphorn Biewkhaimuk.

Acharn Teeranat Karnjana-uksorn, who was part of the original research team, had to withdraw because of other commitments, but continued to help a great deal with advice and assistance in collecting materials. The research team would like to thank Acharn Teeranat specially for her valuable assistance.

The research team also received cooperation from many businessmen, civil servants and academicians outside the Faculty. Special thanks are due to Khun Krairong Navigkaphon, Khun Kittidet Sutsukhon, Khun Rudee Jiwalak, Dr Chris Baker, Khun Chaiyachet Sunthornphiphit, Khun Prinya Sri-thup, Khun Apilas Osathanon, Khun Bulthawat Sisinghasongkhram, Assistant Professors Sombat Chantornvong, Dr Gothom Areeya, Dr Withaya Sucharitthanarak, Dr Somboon Suksamran, Dr Prisadang Chuphen, Dr Direk Pathamasiriwat, Dr Somchai Pakkapatwiwat, Dr Tin Pratchayapruk, Dr Anek Laothamatas.

Several police and military officers gave invaluable advice, particularly Police Lieutenant General Wasit Dejkunchorn and Police Major General Seri Temiyavej.

A special debt of thanks is due to the several thousand unnamed people who gave interviews, participated in the focus groups, attended workshops, and filled in the survey questionnaires. Thanks go to Acharn Buaphan Phaktham of Khon Kaen University, Khun Suwit Watnu, Khun Pitcha Kaewkhao, Khun Suganya Pornsophakun and her husband who helped coordinate the collection of the questionnaires in the northeast, east, south and north respectively.

We owe a debt of gratitude to all those who gave moral support when the Chart Thai Party threatened to sue for libel over the results of the questionnaire survey, including the Rector, Dean of the Faculty of Economics and the University Councillors of Chulalongkorn University; members of media especially Khun Suthichai Yoon, Khun Supap Kleekrajai, Acharn Kasemsan Virakul, Khun Sophon Ongkan, Khun Jitraporn Wanatphong, Khun Chawarong Limpathamapani, Radio Chula, Radio Thailand, TV Channel 5; and many other colleagues and members of the public.

Special thanks are due to Dr. Richard N. Blue, Khun Saneh Ratachinda and the Asia Foundation for financial assistance for the study and for the publication of both Thai and English versions of the research results.

Many helped with the preparations of the study and the manuscripts. We would like to thank Acharn Duangmanee Laovakul, Khun Supaporn Trongkitwirote, Khun Khomsan Minpairote, Khun Nalinee Sikasikul, Khun Benjamat Chumworathayi, Khun Nawarat Naepchit, Khun Warajit Sochom, Khun Wimonrat Sukcharoen, Khun Sombat Saehae, Khun Korakot Muangthai, Khun Wannee Wiwathanapirak, Khun Chofa Jetanaweraput. Many thanks also to several M.A. students who helped with the organization of seminars and workshops.

Finally, thanks are due to Dr Kanchada Piriyarangsan who has given warm and consistent moral support for Sungsidh's work, and to Narote Piriyarangsan, Sungsidh's two year old son who is the happiness and the hope of the family.

The original Thai version of this study appeared under the title *Khorrapchan kap prachathippatai thai* in June 1994. The English version of 1994 is slightly shorter. Due to space limitations, we have omitted the appendices of chapter 1, tables from the questionnaire survey and focus groups, the review of literature, and the chapter on anti-corruption laws.

The research team would like to dedicate this study to Thai society. The research team welcomes any comments, suggestions and criticisms from the readers.

Pasuk Phongpaichit
Sungsidh Piriyarangsan

July 1994

CORRUPTION
AND
DEMOCRACY
IN
THAILAND

1
GIFT CHEQUES AND
GIN MUANG

Corruption in Thai politics is nothing new. Corruption charges
and corruption cases have been an intermittent feature of the Thai
political scene for many years. In the recent past, there have been
some spectacular revelations of political corruption, particularly
in the aftermath of the fall of authoritarian leaders (Sarit,
Thanom-Praphat).[1] But what is especially interesting about the
Thai case since the late 1980s is the rapidly growing prominence
of corruption *as a political issue*. In this chapter the *issue* of
corruption is explored as a way to analyse the nature of Thai
politics in its current stage.

This involves asking two related questions. First, why has
corruption become such a prominent issue at the present time?[2]
If one were to confront the question of corruption five years ago,
it would have appeared as a feature of Thai politics in common
with many other countries, but hardly as a political *issue*. Yet
throughout 1988 and 1989, the parliament devoted a large part of
its time to debating no-confidence motions brought on grounds of
corruption. In 1991, the military junta cited corruption as a major
justification for overthrowing the government by coup.[3] Several
of the pre-coup ministers were subsequently declared 'unusually
rich' for having received improbable numbers of gift cheques
from businessmen involved in government-awarded contracts
and licences.[4] Subsequently the military junta's branding of the
pre-coup politicians as 'unusually rich' was declared

unconstitutional, but revelations concerning corrupt practices have continued to be a key part of the political scene.

Second, what is the relationship between the corruption issue and democratization? The relationship is clearly complex. The military junta which carried out the 1991 coup justified their seizure of power and dismissal of parliament as a move to counter corruption *in order to save democracy*. In response, the civilian politicians opposed to military rule hinted broadly at military corruption over arms sales, and drew attention to some unusually large investments made by a leader of the coup junta.[5] One of the politicians originally branded as 'unusually rich' by the National Peace Keeping Council (NPKC), was suddenly declared innocent and promptly named leader of a military-backed political party, Samakkhitham. Several others on the list of 'unusually rich' subsequently followed the same route. When the coup leaders formed a government in April 1992, three of those they had accused of becoming 'unusually rich' a year earlier were offered posts in the cabinet. Corruption has become a key variable in the debate on who should rule, and how fast and how far the nation should progress along the road to democracy. Yet members of the military junta which made the coup against the elected government in February 1991 on grounds of corruption, were themselves tainted with the suspicion of corruption and were quite prepared to make political deals with people they had only recently branded as corrupt.

This chapter starts out by reviewing past studies of corruption in Thai politics and administration. Then with this background it moves on to analyse why corruption has become an issue in Thai politics at the present time. Finally it returns to examine the impact of the corruption issue on the development of democratic politics.

Studies of corruption in Thailand

There is a relatively extensive literature on corruption in Thailand extending back several decades. But this literature is concerned almost exclusively with the cultural roots of corruption in Thai administration and politics. This focus stems in part from the apparent pervasiveness of corruption within the Thai bureaucratic and political systems. In a study published in 1975, for instance, Morell showed that at least 75 per cent of MPs received commissions from development projects and payments from party leaders in return for their support, and many also may have been involved in extorting money from local businessmen. Morell estimated that corruption by members of the legislatures generated income flows in the range of US$ 0.4 to 1.7 million per year. Yet he contended that this amount was small in comparison to the income flows from corruption in the bureaucracy. He estimated that between 1969 and 1971 bureaucratic corruption may have involved up to US$ 800 million or half of the government budget.[6]

Many of the writers on corruption in Thai politics since the Second World War start out from the seminal article by Lucien Hanks on 'Merit and Power in the Thai Social Order'.[7] Hanks argued that within the Thai value system, merit could be derived from power and that this equation was the basis for patron-client relationships which formed the structure of Thai political society. Following Hanks, subsequent writers interpreted Thai political corruption in the context of patron-client ties.

Writing in the 1960s, Fred W. Riggs[8] analysed the ways in which the Chinese business community was able to flourish in Thailand. Each businessman received protection from an influential Thai official to carry out his business, and in return the Chinese businessman paid his protector or patron for the service.[9] Riggs argued that in the traditional context of Thai society this exchange of mutual interests—an exchange of money for political protection—was a normal state of affairs and should not be considered a corrupt practice.

Van Roy[10] explained the existence and continuity of pervasive corruption in Thailand as a carryover of patron-client style relationships from the pre-modern *sakdina*[11] period, and especially from the Thai tradition of presenting gifts to high officials. Once appointed to a senior position, a Thai bureaucrat will tend to treat his office as a private domain and as a legitimate tool for generating revenue. He will accept fees and gifts for services rendered. He will collect various taxes and royalties, and feel justified in keeping a portion for himself as long as a requisite or reasonable amount is remitted to the state. Van Roy noted that some more modernized and western-educated Thai officials had started to apply western norms and to label certain exchanges of money and privilege as corrupt, but concluded that this criticism was peripheral and that such exchanges were deep-rooted in Thai traditional culture.

Corruption persists, Van Roy concluded, because political institutions which can supersede traditional practices are slow to develop. He went on to argue that such traditionally derived practices had a positive functional effect within the context of the rapid pace of change experienced by Thai society. He thus concluded that 'substantial documentation supports the functionalist premise that corruption maintains systemic stability and continuity by making behavioral boundaries congruent with a well-established morality'.

Thinapan Nakata also saw patron-client relations as one of the major causes of corruption. His findings further showed that the problem of bureaucratic corruption involves incongruities between the legal codes based on western models, and traditional social norms which tolerate corruption.[12]

Clark Neher[13] developed this approach more fully. Following Hanks, he started from the premise that acceptance of a hierarchical order is the basis of patron-client relationships and the central pillar of political culture. The patron-client structure exists and continues to exist because everyone concerned sees it as a good structure which brings benefits in terms of stability, order and the resolution of potentially destabilizing conflicts. The patron-client relationship continues to be important because institutions which bridge between the people and the state (parliaments, political parties) are still weak. The patron-client relationship connects the officials to the people and is the most organized system to allocate social gains and interests. The patron-client relationship flourishes in a society where there is no equality in property, status and power. Little people must find a patron and offer respect, gifts and services in order to ensure favour and security. Big people try to build up their clientele in order to maximize the flow of gifts and favours. People in high office must generate enough money to provide resources and protection for their followers in order to maintain their loyalty in the context of keen competition among different factions. The more followers one has, the more advantaged one is. Such a system institutionalizes exchanges of money and power which may be classified as corruption—bribery, commission fees, illegal use of political power to make money for private gains, embezzlement of public money.

In Neher's view, competition to secure the corruption revenue that accrues from command of high office is a key theme in Thai politics. Often powerful military figures topple civilian governments and put themselves into power because the civilian government refuses to let them have access to public money. In 1947 the government of Khuang Aphaiwong was toppled because he refused to give military men the financial support they wanted from the government. In 1957 Sarit Thanarat toppled Phibun Songkram soon after Phibun had refused to let him make use of the proceeds of the public lottery for his private ends.

The new political parties, according to Neher, work in the same milieu. To win an election, a party must woo the locally powerful candidates to run under its banner, and that wooing requires money. Once in power, the party (or its leaders) need to recoup their funds, generally at public expense. Additional funds can be generated by selling political favours to businessmen who are only too ready to pay the price.

In sum, several studies on corruption in Thailand have indicated that there is corruption in all levels of the bureaucracy and the political system, and that for many of those involved the practices are legitimate under the patronage system although illegal in the context of modern laws. This conflict between what is legitimate in the traditional culture and what is wrong under the modern legal code has existed in Thai politics for a long time. Thai politicians and Thai élites resolve the conflict by adhering to tradition rather than to the modern standards of official practice.

In addition to the major theme of the cultural origins of corruption, several writers refer to three other factors in the pervasiveness of Thai corruption: the low level of official salaries, the limitations on legal provisions and procedures for policing corruption, and the weakness of public opposition.

Despite a proliferation of laws and commissions on corruption, there are still many areas in which it is possible to circumvent legal restrictions. For instance, commissions on arms purchases are not illegal if they are routed through a third party rather than directly through a military officer involved in the purchasing transaction. Further, many of the procedures for investigating allegations of corruption within the bureaucracy are limited in scope. A large measure of discretion to pursue or not to pursue such investigations is given to department heads and other immediate superiors who may be involved in the same corrupt scheme or at least may not be opposed to it on grounds of principle.

Finally the concept of 'public service' as a counterweight to corruption has limited meaning when the public opposition to corruption is weak or non-existent. The people themselves are confused about what is corrupt and not corrupt. They are also not so clear about the concept of what is public good or public service. There has been little pressure from corporate bodies such as business groups or political parties to limit corruption. This ambivalence can contribute to the persistence of corruption. The public lets corrupt officials get away with it.

The origins of the corruption issue in the 1980s

In the traditional *sakdina* system of government, officials received their appointment from a higher authority but were not remunerated by any flow of income from the same source. They were expected to remunerate themselves by retaining a reasonable portion of the taxes they collected, and by exacting fees for services rendered.

This structure was made quite explicit in the tax-farming systems which became such a dominant part of the administrative system in the mid-nineteenth century. The king subcontracted out the right to collect taxes, and it was assumed that the subcontractor would reserve a portion for personal use.

Similarly provincial governors were expected to remunerate themselves by charging fees for performing their official duties, and perhaps also charging extra fees for bending the rules in such areas as exempting people from performance of the corvée. The equivalent of the minister of trade in Ayutthaya could 'step on the junk' (*khong yieb sampao*) of a private trader and take away some goods as the cost of inspection before allowing the trader to enter the market. These forms of remuneration were supposedly kept within certain conventional limits. For many transactions this limit was 10 per cent, as expressed in the phrase *sip lot nung* (taking one from ten). For tax-farmers, the conventional limit was usually 30 per cent.

Relationships of this kind defined the nature of the administrative system at all levels from the king to the village. The system was maintained by continually incorporating individuals who had successfully managed to set up their own concentrations of wealth and power outside the official ambit. The king would act quickly to build a relationship with emerging warlords by bestowing official titles and establishing (at least in theory) a tributary relationship. Many of the mid-nineteenth century tax-farmers were originally successful traders or local entrepreneurs.

Within this system, concepts of corruption referred to attempts by officials to extract amounts and shares which exceeded the conventional limits. From the point of view of the king, *chor rat bang luang* (literally 'cheating the citizens and hiding from the king') occurred when an official was seen to be diverting too large a share into his own pocket. From the point of view of the people, *gin muang* (literally 'eating the state') occurred when an official (or the king himself) was perceived to be enriching himself abnormally by exploiting the powers of his office. Both these definitions were essentially matters of *degree*. Neither definition challenged the right of the official to divert some portion of taxes and fees for personal use. Indeed, it was accepted that this was how officials were remunerated. It was also accepted that the higher the office, the larger the diversion would be.

The coherence of this system started to be undermined by the administrative reforms begun under King Chulalongkorn from the 1880s onwards. These reforms introduced the idea of a centralized bureaucracy with professional skills, a system of recruitment and promotion, standards of behaviour, disciplinary rules, and remuneration by salary. Over the next thirty years, most of the functions previously carried out by nobles, tax-farmers, tributary chieftains and local satraps were subsumed under the command of the new centralized bureaucracy.

However, there were substantial compromises between the new system and the old which meant that this 'age of reform' was very far from a complete replacement of one 'feudal' administrative system by another 'bureaucratic' one.

First, the new bureaucracy was far from being open and meritocratic. Indeed it remained dominated by members of royal and noble families, especially at the upper levels. Second, the apex of the governmental pyramid was still the king. This ensured that relationships within the bureaucracy were still very largely tinged by the pre-existing royal and feudal culture. Third, the salaries were low—well below what would be required to maintain a high official in a condition befitting the dignity of his position. Together, these factors ensured that at the upper levels of the bureaucracy officials continued to live largely off their private income which might be substantially created by revenue flows generated by the office itself. People by and large continued to accept that they should pay officials directly for services rendered, and that some portion of the fees and taxes which passed through the hands of officials would remain there.

The revolution of 1932 marked another step away from the traditional system. The authors of the new constitution made a point of separating the spheres of the monarchy and the state, and more specifically the income of the king from the income of the state. This opened the way for a concept of public service which encompassed proper handling of public funds. Over time, the impact of the 1932 revolution also reduced the prominent role of royal and noble families in the bureaucracy.

Subsequently there have been various laws enacted and commissions established to define and monitor corrupt behaviour in the bureaucracy. The modern code of conduct for public officials refers to corruption using the traditional phrase *chor rat bang luang* (literally 'cheating the citizens and hiding from the king') and defines it to include extortion, acceptance of bribes, and use of official position for private gain on the part of the official himself or other people.[14] This definition explicitly outlaws gifts taken in return for services or activities which the official has the duty to perform, and the use of official position to grant favours to friends and relatives.

In 1975 the government created *khana kammakan pongkan lae prap pram kan thutjarit lae praphuet mi chop nai wong ratchakan* (the Counter Corruption Commission or CCC for short), popularly known as *po po po*, as a watchdog on corrupt practices by public servants. The law empowered the Commission to monitor two kinds of undesirable activity. In the first type, government officials abuse their position or neglect their duty in ways which result in direct benefits accruing to themselves or others. In the second type, government officials use their position, neglect their duty or bypass official orders *with the intention* to create misuse of public funds, and can be found guilty whether or not they or a third party can be proved to have benefited. This second type is termed 'improper behaviour' (*praphuet mi chob*).[15]

Despite the existence of this legal framework, there is still a very high degree of public acceptance of activities on the part of government officials which are legally defined as corrupt (see below, chapter 5). First, there is large acceptance of the practice of presenting gifts to officials for services rendered, or expected to be rendered, in the course of the official's normal duty. This kind of gift is perceived to be made legitimate in several ways. In part it is a way in which the petitioner can demonstrate his respect for the official's position. In part it can be rationalized as a fee which the official may levy to augment his paltry official salary up to a level which befits the dignity of his office. Both these types of justification have clear elements of a carry-over from the pre-modern system of administration.

Second, there is also some degree of acceptance of activities which enable government servants to profit from the ways in which public funds are distributed or spent. Such profits may come from kickbacks received from contractors, or various kinds of presents and inducements. Again income flows are accepted or at least expected as part of the honour and income-augmenting activity of public office.

Thus despite the transition to a bureaucratic system, there has been considerable carry-over of norms and practices which originated in the pre-modern bureaucratic system and which can be labelled corrupt within the norms and practices of a modern bureaucracy. These practices are accepted as 'part of the culture', largely as a result of compromises in the process of transition from the old regime to the new.

Influences on the modern culture of corruption

At the same time, there have been significant changes occurring both inside and outside the administrative system which have changed the nature and the environment of corruption. These changes include developments within the bureaucracy, changes in the nature of government expenditure, and the growth of electoral politics.

The rise of the military. The most important modern development in the nature of the bureaucracy has been the rise in the position of the military. Following the abolition of the absolute monarchy in 1932, there was no decisive move to erect and legitimize an alternative system for allocating political power. This has resulted in a long history of conflict, experiment and constant rewriting of the constitution. Within this context, the military emerged as one of the major focal points of political power. Military leaders have occupied the prime minister's post for the majority of years since 1932. In addition, the military has disrupted the development of parliamentary politics by a succession of coups, and has successfully retarded the development and acceptance of an alternative power system based on election and parliamentary responsibility.

From their position within the bureaucracy, the military have successfully exploited the ambivalence over the division between public and private funds for both institutional and personal gain. Few people are surprised that senior military officers drive around in luxury cars which, if bought from their official salaries, would take several generations to acquire. Since at least the 1950s, major military figures have appeared prominently on the boards of private companies and there is widespread acceptance of the fact that companies need to build such political links and provide rewards appropriately.

From the 1960s onwards, the military budget expanded very rapidly as a result of the Indochina crisis and the rise of communist insurgency within the country. Initially the United States supplied a large part of the budget required for purchasing modern armaments, but after the American withdrawal in 1975 the total cost fell on the local budget. It is widely believed that arms purchase deals generate large commission payments which constitute a significant portion of the 'black' funds controlled by senior military officers for personal as well as political purposes.

The changing source of corruption revenue. There has been a major change in the nature of the resource flows which the government controls. In the nineteenth century, the channels of *income* flow were very diverse and large numbers of officials were involved in routing this flow and diverting portions of it. By contrast, *expenditure* channels presented fewer opportunities for profit. Government spending was confined to the royal household and a few infrastructure projects such as canal building. The numbers of people involved in routing (and possibly also diverting) these flows were small.

By contrast the twentieth century has seen a rationalization of the *income* channels, and a proliferation and massive growth of *expenditure* channels. As a result, the opportunities for diversion on the expenditure side are now much larger both in number and scale. In particular, as the economy has started to accelerate rapidly, so too have the amounts expended on infrastructural and other development projects. In the mid-1980s, fiscal constraints forced the government to contract out a large number of new infrastructure projects notably in telecommunications and highways to the private sector, while still controlling the bidding process and retaining control of the project via partial equity participation. The new privatization policies open up more avenues for corruption money in the forms of kickbacks and commission fees.

Diversion of expenditure flows requires different techniques to diversion of income flows. It is likely that these techniques, such as kickbacks from the grant of contracts, command less easy public acceptance than the more discrete diversion of income. Certainly, elements of the process involved—intermediaries, bagmen—suggest some nervousness on the part of those involved.

New players. Since the 1960s, the rapid pace of industrialization and urban growth has created new centres of economic power which are pressing for a role in the political process. For the purposes of this study, they constitute two groups: modern metropolitan business associations, and the new provincial businessmen who have attracted the title of *jao pho* or 'local godfathers'.[16]

The processes which propel modern metropolitan businessmen to want a role in the political process are little different from those operating elsewhere. As their businesses become more complex, they find it vital to have political connections and political power in order to defend and promote those interests.

The role of the *jao pho* is more complex. As Turton and Sombat have described, these powerful local businessmen and 'fixers' have generally risen by a combination of aggressive entrepreneurship coupled with local political patronage to exploit new profit-making opportunities emerging as a result of the expanding economy.[17] A typical *jao pho* controls a range of businesses including retail, services and low-tech manufacturing, most of which have been buoyed up by expanding local demand. The success of the *jao pho* has often lain in his ability to develop mutually beneficial relationships with local officialdom and use those links to play a crucial intermediary role between the state and a wide array of local interests.

For both the *jao pho* and many modern businessmen, politics is very much part of business. It is part of building the network of contacts needed for doing business. It is also a business in itself. The bureaucrats have demonstrated how political power can be used to make profit. As profit-seeking entrepreneurs, these businessmen are responding to the demonstration effect.

Within a nineteenth-century system, the *jao pho* would be the kind of local satraps which the state would want to pull into the system by granting them an official position and demanding some portion of their profits in return for the grant of legitimacy. Within the late twentieth-century system, this kind of adoption is not so simple.

Both modern business and the *jao pho* have seen electoral politics as a route towards political power. Since the 1970s, these two groups have been prominent in the movement to expand the role of electoral and parliamentary politics. They have been heavily involved in forming political parties, pressing for constitutional reform, electioneering, and the formation of cabinets within a parliamentary system.

Since the mid-1970s, representatives of these groups have gradually assumed a growing role in government. In the cabinets of the so-called 'democratic period' of 1973-76, they made their first major appearance, but were then pushed back into the background by the 1976 coup and the period of conservative reconstruction. Then through the succession of governments headed by General Prem in the early and mid-1980s, they took an increasing role. Finally, after a constitutional change and the election of 1988, a government was installed which was widely recognized as representative of business interests. The cabinet included several members who were easily identifiable as *jao pho* and several who were representative of Bangkok's modern business community.

This parliament was far from being in untrammelled command of the country, for the palace, the military and the bureaucracy still existed as significant centres of power. But the appearance of ministers, and especially of a prime minister, whose ascent was based on popular election and who derived virtually none of their legitimacy from bureaucratic position, royal favour or other sources of traditional legitimacy, presented a new element in the political spectrum.

The corruption issue. Corruption became the dominating issue of the elected government in power from August 1988 to February 1991. The ministry faced several no-confidence debates, in which the proponents focused almost solely on the alleged corrupt practices of various ministers and their friends. When the government was brought down by a coup in February 1991, corruption was cited by the military coup-makers as one of the key justifications, and it quickly became the only justification. One of the first acts of the coup regime was to set up an Assets Committee to investigate 25 ministers and their associates for corruption. Thirteen out of the 25 individuals (including prime minister Chatichai, his personal aide, and other cabinet ministers) were found to be 'unusually wealthy'. The Assets Committee ordered confiscation of altogether about 1.9 billion baht of their assets. The most important evidence found by the commission against these politicians was large numbers of gift cheques presented by businessmen involved in government-licensed or government-contracted businesses.

There were several key features of this chain of events. First, the focus was on corruption by elected politicians rather than appointed officials. Second, the amounts of money alleged or rumoured to be involved in each case of corruption were very large. Third, the incidents which were cited all concerned diversion of *expenditure* flows—particularly irregularities in the allocation of major infrastructure contracts. Fourth, most of the politicians involved were clearly identifiable as *jao pho* or representatives of modern business.

Corruption and democracy

Almost 30 years earlier, in 1963, another corruption scandal had emerged. The public learned that Sarit Thanarat, the military ruler who had recently died, had diverted around 2,784 million baht (approximately US$ 140 million) from public funds for his private use.[18] In today's term this would amount to some 80 billion baht. Sarit's corruption had continued for many years without public knowledge and was revealed only after his death. During Sarit's lifetime few people were aware of the extent of this corruption. The military domination of government ensured that the corruption money was not only controlled within a small group of appointed politicians and bureaucrats, but was also hidden from public knowledge.

The recent change in the political system in Thailand from a bureaucratic polity to a more democratic one has important implications on the nature and scale of corruption. And the issue of corruption has important implications for the development of democracy.

The progress of industrialization and economic development is having two related effects on the processes of corruption. First, it is increasing the potential corruption revenue. Second, it is increasing the level of competition to control this revenue.

Under the bureaucratic polity, bureaucrats including the military were in a position to monopolize the revenue from corruption. Of course there would be competition among individuals and groups within the bureaucracy, but these could be settled by time-honoured techniques of factional alliance, negotiation, and compromise. The rise of business groups has brought in a new kind of competitor. Through elections, parliamentary seats, and ministerial office they have gained access to opportunities to obtain corruption revenue in various ways.

For the new politicians, the revenue from corruption is often a crucial element in building their political base. Political parties are still institutionally weak and have no methods for public collection of support funds. Elections require major expenses both for above-the-board campaigning and for other purposes. Once in office, a politician must be able to maintain a flow of funds to his supporters and constituents in order to prove his worth and consolidate his chances of re-election. New politicians clearly seek revenues from corruption to help finance this expensive political base-building.

Established bureaucrats oppose this diversion of revenues from corruption for several reasons. First, they resent the capture of revenues which traditionally might have been channelled to them. Second, they do not wish to give the new politicians a chance to use these funds to consolidate their power base, to become even stronger in the future, and to become even more effective in monopolizing the revenue from corruption.

In a similar way, the new business politicians have deliberately mounted attacks on the revenue from corruption which flows to the bureaucracy, and particularly to the military. They see the importance of cutting off the resource flows which the military can use for building, consolidating, and defending their prominent role in the polity. From the mid-1980s onwards, the civilian politicians used parliament to mount attacks on the military budget and in particular to reduce the subventions for abnormal arms purchases.[19]

The coup of February 1991 took place precisely within this context of competition over revenues from corruption. In the weeks immediately preceding the coup, several major infrastructure projects were awarded amidst rumours of very large sums being paid to the businessmen politicians holding the ministeral posts which oversaw the contracts. Only days before the coup, the cabinet refused to pass a military subvention for special arms purchases. Then immediately after the coup, the military-led government started investigations designed to freeze and seize politicians' assets which could be shown to have been corruptly acquired. The military also quickly posted a series of requests for arms purchases which were later described as the biggest arms shopping spree the nation had ever seen.

The military which has been involved in time-honoured forms of bureaucratic corruption is unhappy about the intrusion of new power groups which may be getting better access and using better techniques to garner the revenue from corruption. The contest is not only about sharing the corruption money, but it is also about the balance of political power. By permitting the new power groups to have access to corruption money, the military believe they will eventually lose control over the political process. The new power groups will have a free hand to build up political parties and will be able to use party organization and mass support to suppress the military and the old order. An established parliamentary system will shift political power away from the military.

The basic conflict between the military and the new politicians over relative power and competitive access to revenues from corruption does not rule out the possibility of short-term alliances and factional alignments which cut across the military-politician divide. Indeed in the aftermath of the 1991 coup, the military successfully brought in several business politicians to help man the interim cabinet. The military leaders also negotiated with several other politicians to form a political party which would support military aims after the restoration of parliamentary rule. Some of the politicians under investigation by the junta's anti-corruption commission joined this party within days of being declared not guilty of corruption. The new party attracted several prominent *jao pho* and some leading members of the government which the military leaders had only recently overthrown. Alliances and compromises of this kind are a normal day-to-day feature of the political system. But they do not change the structural base of competition between the military concerned to preserve its power base and revenues from corruption which are under attack, and the new politicians attempting to gain access to revenues from corruption to consolidate and extend the growing power base of their own.

There are already signs that military leaders are searching for new strategies to preserve the position of the military, or even to remodel it for the future. First, there have been attempts to develop new sources of revenue which are not vulnerable to attack and control by politicians and parliament in the manner of the arms budgets. One strategy has been to find ways to mobilize the landed assets which the military now controls, and make them available for quasi-commercial development under military management. Second, some military leaders have looked at playing the political game at least partially within the rules laid down by the emerging democratic structure. Since the mid-1980s, several leading military figures have made the transition to electoral politics. In 1991, General Chavalit, the previous commander-in-chief, left the army and formed a new nationwide political party to contest the elections. Following the coup, the military leaders sponsored the formation of a political party with a platform of defending military interests within the democratic process. Third, the military leaders have initiated internal research and debate on mapping options for the future course for the military, including options which would mark a significant withdrawal from the political arena.

The rise of the corruption issue might be imagined to have some impact on popular attitudes towards democracy and democratic processes. The coup leaders invested considerable efforts in portraying the previous civilian government as unusually corrupt. In the run-up to the March 1992 elections for a new parliament, the military leaders orchestrated a campaign to draw attention to vote buying and other forms of corruption in the election process.

The polls in March and September 1992, however, gave little evidence of growing disaffection with democratic processes. The polls were hotly contested. Campaign strategies and voting patterns followed party lines to a larger degree than in previous elections. The percentage turnouts were high in relation to previous elections.

There was, however, a very clear difference in voting preference between Bangkok and the rest of the country. In the March election, Bangkok voters plumped overwhelmingly for the political leader (Chamlong) who promoted himself as a Mr Clean, whose campaign visual was a cartoon of himself holding a broom, and who campaigned on the basis of his corruption-free track record as mayor of Bangkok.[20] His party won 32 of the 35 seats in the capital. Upcountry voters still largely selected their local *jao pho*. This could be interpreted in many ways, including the continued importance of money at the polling booth. However to some extent it demonstrates the continued desire of the upcountry voter to cast his vote for a 'big man', partly as a token of respect for his local power, partly in the hope that he would be powerful enough to bring benefits back from Bangkok to the locality.

Perspective and conclusion

Writing in the early years of the American revolution, James Madison and Alexis de Tocqueville both confronted the central paradox of the theory of democracy: among the freedoms protected by the democratic ideal is the freedom to destroy democracy itself.

De Tocqueville in particular wanted to understand the components of democracy and to assess those forces that might enhance or diminish its prospects. He discussed political corruption in the United States as part of his treatment of the socio-economic forces that made democracy possible in a new nation. He stressed that the relative inequality of conditions urged men to embark on commerce and industry, and this in turn redistributed wealth and property. He believed that this process was the core of American liberal democracy. But he was concerned that such tendencies contained the potential conditions which might ultimately undermine and corrupt democratic institutions. Economic progress could lead to concentration of economic, social and political power and so to political corruption by the powerful to maintain their power.[21]

Since the 1960s, political scientists studying the development of democratic institutions in new states have confronted the same paradox.[22] Huntington, a key figure in the 'modernization' school, pointed out that corruption was a feature of the United Kingdom and the United States during the height of each country's modernizing periods, namely in the eighteenth century in the United Kingdom and in the nineteenth century in the United States. Along with Scott and others, Huntington argued that the modernization process increases the incidence of corruption for four major reasons. First, in many pre-modern societies patronage, favouritism and the appropriation of public funds for personal use were acceptable and legitimate forms of behaviour. The distinction between the king's purse and the public coffers was blurred. During and after the transition to modern institutions of bureaucracy and parliament, these traditional practices persisted.

Second, the process of modernization actually increased the potential for corrupt practices. With modernization, new norms were introduced and many of the old legitimate ways were subject to new standards. In this transition period, many people became confused over the issue of public and private domains. This confusion gave opportunities for people to get away with all kinds of corrupt behaviour—including behaviour which was unacceptable by either old or new standards.[23]

Third, people with new wealth used that wealth to buy power, often by bribing and in other ways buying over the nobles, landlords or bureaucrats who dominated the old order. Conflict could arise because of the attempts by the old élites to block the growth of the new wealth, or simply because the outdated bureaucratic system could not adjust and cope readily with the demands of the new wealth. People with new wealth who found that the legitimate routes to political power were blocked by vested interests or arcane procedures resorted to buying their way into parliament or political office. Corruption thus became a technique for 'new men' to overcome their alienation from the political process and achieve political participation equivalent to their wealth and economic power.

Fourthly, modernization processes in newly independent nations or in newly developing countries went hand in hand with an expansion of the state apparatus in the economic and social spheres. This invariably led to an increase in bureaucratic control on economic activities which tended to increase costs and reduce profitability of business undertakings. More controls meant more corruption. More legal sanctions against corruption at this stage might further increase opportunities for corruption by inflating the 'black' economy.

Huntington also traced the links between corruption and political instability. When politicians are seen using money power to secure support or to control the behaviour of individuals, or when politicians are seen to be enriching themselves from public funds rather than executing the public projects which they have promised, the decline in public confidence can open the way for coups, revolts and other forms of violent change.[24] Corruption is often cited by the military as a reason to topple civilian governments and establish military rule. This is particularly relevant to developing countries where the military still operates as an important political institution.

However Huntington suggested that some types of corruption may strengthen political parties and in the long run lead to political development. He pointed out that in Europe and the United States in the early stages of industrialization and democratic development, governments were vulnerable to military intervention and military overthrow. This situation prompted civilian politicians to develop stronger political parties as a counterweight to military power. In the early stages, various forms of corrupt practice—Tammany Hall, pork barrel—were important in building up the structure and the assets to make political parties strong and effective. In other words Huntington and others argued that while democracy breeds corruption among political parties and politicians in the short term, in the long term democracy allows strong political parties to develop as a means to counter corruption.

The literature on corruption in Thailand has concentrated on the cultural origins of corruption in an attempt to explain the apparent pervasiveness of corruption within the Thai bureaucracy. This literature has argued strongly that activities condemned as corrupt by western norms of public service may be considered as quite legitimate within the framework of Thai patron-client relations, and thus the pervasiveness of so-called corruption is unremarkable.

The sudden upsurge of corruption as a major political issue in the late 1980s and early 1990s appears to contradict the conclusions of the earlier Thai literature. It points to the necessity of studying the political and economic background of corruption, rather than drawing universal conclusions based on cultural analyses.

The rising prominence of business politicians has created a battleground over the control of revenue from corruption. The protagonists are the military, who represent the most politically active segment of the bureaucracy which monopolized the income from corruption in the past, and the new business politicians, who have pressed for greater democratization as a way to insert themselves into positions which give access to the revenue from corruption. The battle is not simply over control of the revenue from corruption itself, but over the ability of each side to deploy this revenue to consolidate its relative political power.

The United States, Japan and European countries passed through stages of tightening the laws against corruption and limiting the political impact of wealth through legislation concerning political donations and campaign funds. However, these moves came only after long periods in which corruption was a political issue. While the trend in Thailand may be expected to move towards this same direction, we may not expect to see much progress within a decade. As long as the military remains powerful as an institution, we shall also see it attempting to garner the revenue from corruption in competition with politicians. The military may even retard the move towards more systematic control of corruption.

To the extent that in Thailand the military tends to stand for a more closed political system, and elected politicians for a more open one, there are grounds to conclude that it is more harmful to have a society being dominated by an honest military than to have a parliamentary system with corrupt politicians. At least under a democratic framework there is the possibility of developing a civil society with the will to control corruption. A more democratic political system allows room for the civil society to learn by experience, to come to understand the concept of public service, and to learn how to exert pressure against corrupt practices.

The military has raised the corruption issue as an excuse for its attempts to retard democratic development while it searches round for new strategies to conserve its political position in the long term. In the long run, however, the checks and balances of a full democratic system and the development of a civil society will prove a more effective means to control corruption than the intervention of a man on a white horse. For the moment it appears that the Thai electorate agrees with this conclusion.

Notes

1. After the death of Sarit in 1963, it was discovered that he had amassed 2.8 billion baht, roughly equivalent to 80 billion at today' value, or 26 per cent of the actual government expenditure in 1990. Sources: Corruption figures from Siamwalla (1992). The government expenditure figures are from the Bank of Thailand, *Quarterly Bulletin*, March 1990, Table 24.

2. In August 1988 Prime Minister Chatichai became the first elected Thai prime minister for 12 years. The majority of his cabinet members were also chosen from elected MPs.

3. The National Peace-Keeping Council (NPKC) set up by the military junta who engineered the coup on 23 February 1991 cited five reasons for the coup against the Chatichai administration: government corruption, harassment by political officials against honest permanent officials, 'parliamentary dictatorship', attempts to destroy the military institution, and moves to distort a court case involving attempts to topple the monarchy.

4. Thirteen out of 25 individuals (including Prime Minister Chatichai, his personal aide, and other cabinet ministers) targeted for investigation by the Assets Committee, were found to be 'unusually wealthy'. The Assets Committee ordered confiscation of altogether some 1.9 billion baht of their gift cheques and other assets. Just before the election in March 1992, two ex-cabinet ministers were absolved of the charge of having become unusually rich. One of the two, Narong Wongwan, later headed the military-backed political party Samakkhitham. At the March 1992 elections, Samakkhitham won the largest number of seats, and Narong was set to be the premier. But an American official confirmed a report that Narong was once refused a visa to the United States on the grounds of his alleged involvement in narcotics. Narong had to step aside and General Suchinda Kraprayun, leader of the coup of 1991, was presented as premier instead. Suchinda subsequently had to resign from the premiership following the protest against his appointment and the May Incident of 1992. In September 1992 another election was called. This time the Democrat Party won the largest number of seats and headed the coalition government. The politicians whose assets had been seized then appealed to the high court to declare the seizure unlawful. In March 1993 the high court ruled in favour of the ten politicians who had their asset seized. The NPKC's establishment of the investigative Assets Committee was declared unconstitutional, and against the jural tradition of Thailand. The Assets Committee had no right to act as a court. The case of the unusually rich should have been decided in the court of law, rather than by an ad hoc committee. While the high court's ruling set aside the action of the military junta, it said nothing about whether the 10 cabinet ministers were clear of their corruption charges. See the Announcement of the NPKC No. 26

concerning the seizure of assets; the name list of 'the unusually rich' politicians; and the verdict of the high court declaring 'the seizure of assets' unconstitutional in Pasuk and Sungsidh (1994: Appendices).

5. See a detailed analysis of the controversy over the military budget in Thai politics in the late 1980s in Phongpaichit (1992).

6. D. Morell 'Legislatures and Political Development: The Problem of Corruption', paper read at the Conference on Legislatures in Contemporary Societies, Albany, New York, January 1975, quoted in Neher (1988: 283).

7. Hanks (1962).

8. Riggs (1966).

9. Riggs (1966: 251).

10. Van Roy (1970).

11. The term *sakdina* refers to the system of aristocrat-officials which existed under the monarchy from roughly the sixteenth to nineteenth centuries.

12. Thinapan (1977).

13. Neher (1977).

14. Office of the Prime Minister (1977).

15. See further details about the setting up of the CCC and anti-corruption laws which governs it in Pasuk and Sungsidh (1994: 342-366).

16. See detailed discussion on *jao pho* in chapter 3 below.

17. Turton (1989); Sombat (1992).

18. Thak (1979: 335-337). This was the amount of Sarit's wealth which his children claimed Wichitra, Sarit's last wife, tried to hide away from them. Additional wealth was said to be in the form of many intangibles which could not be accounted for. See below chapter 2.

19. See Phongpaichit (1992).

20. From April-May 1992 onwards, the image of Chamlong and the Palang Dharma party became significantly more complex. But at the March polls, Chamlong and his party still mainly stood for clean politics.

21. See a discussion of Madison and Alexis de Tocqueville on corruption in Berg (1976: 6-14).

22. Huntington (1968); Scott (1972).

23. Gunnar Myrdal also discussed the effects of traditional norms on corruption. But he put it slightly differently. Myrdal argued that modern practice of gift-giving to secure favour for private interests was a distortion of the traditional practice and contrary to traditional norms and standards (Myrdal, 1968). Several writers on Thailand, however, have pointed out that in the traditional Thai context gift-giving was a legitimate means to secure favour (Riggs, 1966;

Scott, 1972; Van Roy, 1970). So adhering to this traditional practice may not be considered a distortion of traditional norms. It merely reflects a negation of the modern norms which consider gift-giving for private gains illegitimate. See chapter 5 below on results of the survey on attitudes of the Thai public towards gift-giving and corruption.

24. This happened several times in the past, and again during the premiership of Chatichai Choonhawan (1988-1990). Party leaders can only control their MPs by using money. Once MPs take ministerial office, they use their office to collect funds for the party, and for their supporters. Ministers take gifts and bribes from big businesses. The public starts to lose confidence. This makes it possible for the military to step in and use corruption charges as one of the reasons for a coup.

2
HOW MUCH?
FROM SARIT TO CHATICHAI

Corruption among leading politicians became a major issue after the death of Field Marshal Sarit Thanarat. Sarit became prime minister following a military coup staged in 1957, and died while still in office in 1963. His military regime was described as dictatorial and repressive.[1] After his death, disputes among his heirs uncovered the spectacular extent of Sarit's personal fortune. In court, as noted in the previous chapter, it was revealed that Sarit's wealth at the time of his death amounted to 2.8 billion baht. The publicity of the court case forced the government to investigate the sources of Sarit's great wealth. It was found that Sarit had used government funds to maintain his mistresses and invest in business. Sarit and his wife had interests in 45 companies, held numerous stock holdings and bank accounts, and owned almost nine thousand acres of land.[2] The investigation reckoned that the three major sources of this wealth were approximately 394 million baht taken from the Secret Investigation Fund of the Prime Minister's Office, 240 million baht from the Lottery Bureau, and about 100 million baht from a percentage cut on the sale of lottery tickets.[3] The government had sufficient evidence to seize assets worth 604 million baht from Sarit's family. This represented about 20 per cent of his estimated total wealth.

Ten years later the government led by Sarit's political heirs, prime minister Thanom Kittikachorn, General Praphat Charusathian, and Colonel Narong Kittikachorn, were ousted and subsequently investigated for corruption. In this case the government had evidence to seize assets totalling 600 million baht from the three military men and their families.

From 1981 to 1988, while the prime ministership was held by General Prem Tinsulanond, there was no incident of scandalous political corruption. In 1988, Chatichai Choonhawan became the first elected MP to hold the prime ministership since 1976. Corruption among leading politicians again became a big issue. In this period, the Thai economy went through an unprecedented boom. The government pushed ahead with many large infrastructure projects, each involving several billion baht. There were widespread rumours about kickbacks given to ministers by firms which won bids for these large contracts. Some government officials appointed by the Chatichai government were allegedly involved in the bidding for government projects in state enterprises, and in defalcation of foreign aid funds for refugees. Some military officers and associates were alleged to have received commissions from arms purchases.

The wide publicity of these cases gave the impression that corruption was more widespread under an elected government than under the dictatorial governments of Sarit and Thanom, or under the 'demi-democracy' of the Prem period. The military junta called the National Peace Keeping Council (NPKC) which staged the coup against prime minister Chatichai in February 1991, cited corruption as one of the major causes of the power seizure. Following the coup, a special committee set up by the NPKC declared that Chatichai, his aide and eight ministers had become 'unusually wealthy' during their time in office. The committee ordered the seizure of assets totalling 1,900 million baht belonging to 10 politicians, on grounds that they were acquired corruptly. After the re-establishment of the parliament in 1992, the high court ruled that the seizure of the assets of the 10 politicians was against the constitution. The assets were subsequently returned to the previous owners. However, the high court ruling said nothing about whether these assets were acquired honestly or not.

During the Chatichai period and the NPKC regime, the publicity surrounding corruption by *elected* politicians completely overshadowed reports of corruption within the permanent bureaucracy, with one exception. Because of the real estate boom in this period, the Land Department appeared prominently in the news in matters relating to bureaucratic corruption. The real estate boom gave rise to numerous land transfers, and many opportunities for corruption among the officials of the Land Department.

This chapter attempts to compare corruption among politicians and bureaucrats, and to see whether it is possible to say that elected governments are more corrupt than dictatorial governments. Statistics compiled from official records of corruption cases will be used to make the estimate. Comparisons will be made of the major patterns of corruption practised in different regimes.

Corruption among politicians and bureaucrats take many different forms. Many types of 'structural' corruption and nepotism are virtually impossible to quantify on account of lack of data. The focus here is on corruption which can be quantified in monetary terms. With regard to bureaucratic corruption, the estimation focuses on leakages out of the government expenditure set by the annual budget. In the case of political corruption, the focus is on cases in which politicians were involved in corruption charges and had their assets seized or frozen. Estimates of corruption among politicians will be based on the value of these seized assts. The last section of the chapter discusses briefly the question of the military and corruption.

Estimates of corruption among bureaucrats

We may distinguish two types of bureaucratic corruption. The first is derived from the use of official positions to extort money. This money does not necessarily come from the government expenditure budget, but may indirectly affect the revenue. Examples include the bribes a police officer receives from owners of brothels and gambling dens in return for freedom to operate their illegal businesses, or from drivers in return for not issuing a fine ticket. The second way government officials make use of their official positions to make money is by extracting from the government revenue or expenditure directly. Corruption from the revenue side includes both outright robbery from the government coffers, and also more subtle forms such as undervaluation of land or goods to reduce their tax liability.[4]

The most common forms of corruption on the government's expenditure side are the kickbacks or commission fees which officials receive from government construction projects, purchases of materials, and other projects put out to bid. The kickbacks are usually charged as a percentage of the project cost. In the case of material purchases, the sellers may overcharge the government with the connivance of the officer in charge, who receives some percentage of the difference as kickback. Sometimes the officers may make up documents showing that purchases have occurred, but no goods or fewer goods are delivered. In all these cases of kickbacks and commission fees, the government loses by being overcharged and possibly also by receiving substandard goods.

Statistics on corruption cases reported to the Counter Corruption Commission (CCC) and reports from newspapers suggest a fairly constant trend of bureaucratic corruption over the period 1970-90. The numbers of cases reported per year in 1981-87, the period under prime minister Prem, were slightly fewer than during 1970-72, the period under the prime ministership of Thanom. The average number of cases rose again in the Chatichai period (1989-1990). The ministries of interior, education and agriculture were high in the list for the number of recorded cases of corruption (Table 1).

Table 1. Average annual number of corruption cases among bureaucrats

Ministry	1970-1972	1981-1987	1989-1990
Interior	857	569	710
Agriculture	-	217	249
Education	80	251	242
Communications	39	64	71
Public Health	-	67	77
Prime Minister's Office	182	17	23
Defence	89	72	67
Finance	45	83	74
Industry	16	15	20
Foreign Affairs	-	3	4
Commerce	-	12	18
Justice	-	12	17
Science & Technology	-	5	4
University Affairs	-	45	42
Economic Development	234	-	-
All ministries	1,542	1,432	1,618

Sources: For 1970-1972, as reported in *Siam Rath Daily*, 3 January 1973. The figures are from complaints sent to the Prime Minister's Office, Public Poll Department, Public Relations Department, and the Office of Public Complaints. The figures do not include complaints sent directly to each ministry in the same period. For 1981-1987 and 1989-1990, from Annual Reports of the Counter Corruption Committee, 1982, 1984, 1985, 1987, 1988, 1990.

Some estimate of the extent of corruption in monetary terms can be obtained from statistics reported in the annual report of the Office of Auditor General (OAG) and of the Counter Corruption Commission (CCC). One of the OAG's functions is to make sure that government expenditure is properly used. Each year, the OAG carries out random checks on the accounts of all the government departments in all ministries, and investigates any irregularities. In the late 1980s, the total amount which the OAG uncovered as improper expenditure and demanded restitution averaged around 100 million baht a year. In 1990 the amount peaked at nearly 176 million baht (Table 2).

Table 2. Government funds judged to have been misused or misappropriated as a result of investigations by the Office of Auditor General (million baht)

Ministry/Office	1987	1988	1989	1990
Prime Minister's Office	0.026	0.069	0.197	0.211
Defence	32.651	14.746	21.849	39.144
Finance	0.009	0.067	1.856	1.686
Foreign Affairs	0.115	0.001	1.243	0.450
Agriculture	0.159	0.154	18.272	11.895
Communications	0.801	3.388	10.871	9.034
Commerce	0.002	0.016	0.085	0.122
Interior	6.508	5.099	8.251	6.998
Justice	0.026	0.482	0.206	0.022
Science & Technology	0.008	0.124	0.891	1.291
Education	1.086	2.507	12.120	8.171
Public Health	1.336	0.162	7.255	6.143
Industry	0.264	0.005	42.174	30.584
University Affairs	4.505	1.160	0.185	3.919
National Assembly	-	-	0.012	0.013
Royal Academy	0.001	-	-	-
Bureau of Royal Households, Grand Palace	-	0.006	0.008	-
Provincial Administration	0.095	2.921	1.431	0.680
Municipalities & Sanitary Districts	4.145	1.781	0.880	2.290
Bangkok Municipality	0.018	0.109	0.191	0.172
State Enterprises	6.017	0.233	8.287	52.724
Regional Offices	45.113	45.684		
Others	5.845			
Total	108.729	78.726	131.845	175.536

Note: These are cases in which the OAG identified irregularity, improper use of funds, dishonesty causing damage to the government, and the amount of money involved. Source: The Office of Auditor General, Annual Reports, 1987-1990.

The reports of the OAG classify corruption sums by ministry. The ministries which had the largest amounts were: defence (especially 1987 and 1990); industry (especially 1989 and 1990); state enterprises (especially 1990); the ministry of agriculture (in 1989 and 1990); and regional offices (in 1987 and 1988).

The reports of the CCC record the sums identified in bureaucratic corruption. In 1986, 1990, 1991, 1992 the amounts involved were very high: 318, 255, 475 and 1265 million baht respectively (Table 3). The high amount in 1992 came mostly from corruption within the Land Department, involving the issuing of fake land title deeds.[5]

Table 3. Amount of money involved in corruption cases investigated by the Counter Corruption Commission (million baht)

Type of Case	1986	1987	1988	1989	1990	1991	1992
1. Corruption	27.5	7.2	4.1	1.9	0.5	2.4	10.1
(number of cases)	*(65)*	*(39)*	*(13)*	*(21)*	*(16)*	*(13)*	*(1)*
2. Unusually rich	213.5	6.7	0.7	18.9	16.0		
(number of cases)	*(1)*	*(1)*	*(1)*	*(2)*	*(4)*		
3. Others	76.9	1.7	50.0	0.1	238.1	472.9	1254.5
(number of cases)	*(6)*	*(3)*	*(1)*	*(2)*	*(1)*	*(3)*	*(7)*
Total	317.9	16.5	54.8	20.9	254.6	475.3	1264.6

Source: *Annual Reports of the Counter Corruption Commission*, 1986-92

The difference between the OAG and the CCC is that the OAG carries out random checks on government departments' accounts as a matter of routine, while the CCC investigates only cases which are reported to them by individuals or government departments.

Because of the lack of comprehensive information, estimation of the extent of bureaucratic corruption is very difficult. However, the cases of corruption reported to the CCC, the OAG, and in the press give a strong impression of the different forms of corruption, and the rough amounts and percentages involved. From this evidence, certain assumptions are made on which estimates can be establised.

The reports of the OAG and the CCC, and interviews with members of parliament and academics who specialize in government budgeting, indicate a wide variety of different leakages on the expenditure side: commission fees and kickbacks from successful bidders for projects; the overpricing of materials and equipment bought for the government; the substandard quality of contract works or equipment bought. The following examples give some indication of the range and the percentages involved. A series of examples taken from newspaper reports in the pre-1976 period is given first.

Purchasing of land for a government department. In 1972, the OAG investigated a notorious case of overpricing in the purchase of three plots of land for the Police Department. A police officer was found guilty of making the government pay 23.4 million baht more than it should, or 52 per cent of the total amount spent.[6]

Investment in infrastructure projects. During 1968-1972, the OAG found irregular payments, improper advance payments, and overpricing in the construction of Sirikit Dam. The amounts involved totalled 200 million baht out of a total expenditure for the project of 1,488 million baht. Of this total amount, 949 million baht came from the annual government budget, and the remainder of 539 million baht was a loan from the World Bank. Expressing the corruption amount of 200 million baht as a per centage of the project allocation from the government budget, the extent of the leakage was 21.1 per cent. If expressed as a percentage of the total project cost the leakage was 13.4 per cent.[7]

Building construction. In 1968 an office of the government mint was built at the cost of 30 million baht. After the construction was completed, the building cracked. It could not bear the weight it was meant to withstand. Investigation showed use of sub-standard materials, and deviations from the design of the architect. Repair of the building cost the government an addition of nearly 10 million baht. As a proportion of the total project cost, this leakage was 33 percent.[8]

Six months after the completion of a school in Bangkok in 1971, cracks appeared on the walls all over the building. On the ground floor one of the main pillars supporting the building cracked. The cost of this building to the government was 1.2 million baht. It was estimated that with an honest contractor such a building could be built to specification with standard quality at the cost of only 700,000 baht. The leakage from overpricing alone was 42 per cent, and rose to over 50 per cent when the repair costs were also included.[9]

Purchase of materials. In a dam construction project in 1970, the irrigation department authorized sixteen orders for purchases of cement in one day. Each purchase authorized the payment of about 250,000 baht. The orders were placed with a cement company in which the director of the Irrigation Department happened to hold a managing directorship. The ordering sixteen times in one day was to get round a rule which stipulated that the director of a department could authorize payments only up to 250,000 baht. It was further found that the amount of the cement delivered was below the amount paid for.

Faking receipts. In 1973 the Governor of Ayutthaya and eight lower officials faked a receipt for 220,000 baht for repairing roads and building welcome gates to receive the official visit of the Queen of England. The investigation revealed that no road was repaired and no welcoming gates were constructed. The corruption in this case was 100 per cent.[10]

In another case in 1975, officials from several government departments made fake claims for subsidies on hospital bills, totalling over 500,000 baht.[11]

In 1975, an official of the energy organization revealed to newspaper reporters that some of the officers in the organization colluded with drivers of government cars to over-report the petrol used. The difference was then shared between the drivers and the officers. It was estimated that the leakage was around 10 per cent.[12]

After 1976, examples of cases are available both in newspaper reports and in the reports of the Counter Corruption Commission.

Purchase of materials. The Express Transport Organization (ETO) is a public enterprise which was responsible for the purchase of asphalt for the Highway Department. In 1985 it was revealed that the ETO had colluded with one asphalt company to make it the sole seller of asphalt to the Highway Department for 15 years. The company overpriced the asphalt which cost the highway department 100-150 million baht extra a year.[13]

A CCC investigation found that for seven years the head pharmacist of a provincial government hospital had bought medicine and hospital equipment from his own company at inflated prices. The overpricing cost the government at least 1.7 million baht.[14]

The CCC found that 150 officers of the Ministry of Education who were responsible for checking the quality of educational materials for local elementary schools all over the country colluded to accept substandard tables and chairs for classrooms. The cost to the government was 3,295,000 baht.[15]

In another case of purchase of educational materials for secondary schools, costing the government 6,565,000 baht, the equipment was later found to be substandard and different from the original specification.[16]

In 1990 the CCC set up a committee to investigate the deputy director of the budget bureau and colleagues who were alleged to be involved in corruption over purchasing of educational equipment for elementary schools. Later the director of the teachers' training department filed a law suit against this group on the charge of colluding to cause the government to buy equipment at inflated cost.[17]

Construction and infrastructure projects. The CCC investigated a complaint that in the repair of a school, costing the government 717,000 baht, the contractor used substandard materials.

Investigation revealed that the contractors used planks which were full of holes from woodworm.[18]

In the construction of housing for teachers in one of the government educational institutions, the construction committee allowed contractors to alter the building and materials specifications in the plans, so that the houses built were not up to standard, causing the government at least 1.2 million baht in damage.[19]

In the construction of five government schools in a province at a total cost of 10.85 million baht, the governor was found to have colluded with the bidder to pay a cost which was inflated by 30 per cent.[20]

Reforestation project. The provincial forestry office contracted a private company to grow seedlings on 3,000 rai of land at the cost of 700 baht per rai. A forestry official signed that the project had been completed and authorized payment of the total amount of 2.1 million baht. Investigation revealed that the company completed the planting on only 2,400 rai of land. The government paid 420,000 too much, representing a leakage rate of 20 per cent.[21]

Compulsory purchase of land. Normally in cases of compulsory purchase of land for irrigation projects, the Irrigation Department uses estimates made by the Land Department to calculate the compensation to be paid to the land owner. In one of these cases, the department officials falsified the documents and overpaid the land owners by 1.9 million baht. The leakage involved was 59 per cent.[22]

Pilferage of government property. An official from the Fishery Department requested 16,000 litres of petrol for use in a department project. Complaints led to an investigation by the CCC, which revealed that 7,000 litres were used for personal matters, while only 9,000 litres were used on official business. The leakage in this case was 44 per cent.[23]

High-ranking officials found to be 'unusually rich'. Anyone who has evidence that a government official may be acquiring assets or wealth 'unusually' can lodge a complaint to the CCC. The CCC may investigate to see if the accusation has any validity. If the result of the investigation suggests that the person may be involved in some corrupt practices causing damage to the government, then the CCC will present the evidence to the official's superior for further appropriate action. If the accused was found to be engaged in corruption which constituted a criminal offence, then his superior must pursue the matter by sending the case to the public prosecutor for legal action.

In the Annual Report of 1986, the CCC reported the case of a high-ranking military officer who was found to have amassed 213.45 million baht without being able to explain where the wealth came from. In another case a middle-level official in charge of the materials section of the Irrigation Office in Nakhon Sithammarat, was found to have acquired assets valued 2.06 million baht between 1978 and 1982. He could not explain the sources of this increased wealth.[24] In another case a middle-level officer of the Department of Irrigation and his wife, an officer of the Ministry of Education, were found to have acquired 7.35 million baht between 1976 and 1983. Neither could explain where their wealth came from. During those years, the husband had been responsible for his section's budget totalling 574.06 million baht. If he had taken the money out of this government budget, then the leakage rate was 1.3 per cent.[25]

Based on examples such as these, we can make certain assumptions. First, most bureaucratic corruption is leakage from the government expenditure on capital projects and on the purchases of goods and services on contract. Hence we shall estimate corruption as a proportion of the sums allocated for these purposes in the budgets of the various departments and ministries. Second, we assume that the leakage rate is 20 per cent. As can be seen from the above cases, the leakage varies a great deal from case to case. It is impossible to calculate the true extent. However, most examples are in the range of 20 to 40 per cent, and hence we have chosen the low end of 20 per cent. Third, we assume that the rate has been constant over this period. The cases given as example show no definite trend, and we can see no reason to assume that there was one either up or down. In sum, we assume that the leakage amounts to a constant 20 per cent of the sums allocated in the department budgets for the purchase of materials or for construction works assigned on contract. We then express this figure as a percentage of the total annual government budget and the GNP to obtain some measure of rates of corruption (Table 4).

Table 4. Estimated value of corruption by bureaucrats (million baht/year)

Ministry	Sarit	Thanom	Sanya-Kriangsak	Prem	Chatichai
	1960-63	1964-73	1974-81	1981-88	1988-90
Interior	20	68	232	430	1148
Agriculture	44	206	720	1566	2194
Education	28	92	352	1102	1072
Communication	68	366	960	1596	2512
Public health	8	32	144	280	364
Others	108	420	1584	2144	4388
Total	272	1180	3996	7120	11676
As % of budget	2.77	5.34	4.93	3.59	4.05
As % of GDP	0.44	0.90	0.84	0.70	0.66

Note: The corruption amount is estimated as 20 per cent of the ministry budget for capital items and purchases of materials and equipment. Total figures may not add up due to rounding.

On these assumptions, the value of corruption among bureaucrats was estimated to be 272 million baht a year in the Sarit period (1957-1963), representing 2.77 percent of the annual budget of the period. The amount rose to 11,676 million baht per year in the Chatichai period (1988-1990), or 4.05 per cent of the annual budget of the same period.

This method of estimating shows high rates of leakage in the Highway and Irrigation departments during the Chatichai period.[26] By way of corroboration, these two departments were specifically cited when corruption issues were debated in the parliament.

The estimated rate of leakage as a percentage of the annual budget rose from around 3 per cent a year in the Sarit period to 5 per cent a year in the Thanom-Praphat, Sanya and Kriangsak periods, and fell to 4 per cent in the Prem and Chatichai periods.

As a percentage of the GDP, the estimated rate of leakage was 0.4 per cent in the Sarit period, rising to 0.9 per cent under Thanom-Praphat, Sanya and Kriangsak. In the Prem and Chatichai periods, the rate fell to around 0.7 per cent per year (Table 4).

Estimates of corruption among politicians

In this section we compare the amounts alleged to have been acquired through corruption by leading politicians in different periods. In the inheritance case, Sarit was found to have total assets of 2.874 billion baht, most of which had apparently been acquired since he wrote his will three years earlier (see below). Eventually 604 million were judged to have been acquired directly from government sources. After the fall of Thanom-Praphat-Narong, the three were accused of having amassed 1 billion baht unlawfully, of which 600 million was eventually proven and seized in restitution. In the Chatichai period, the NPKC committee identified 1.9 billion baht of assets acquired 'unusually' by 10 politicians, including 284 million by Chatichai himself.

For comparison we divide these sums by the number of years these politicians held office, and then express the result as a percentage of the GDP and of the government budget in the respective periods (Tables 5.1 and 5.2).

According to this estimate, in monetary terms the rate of corruption was highest in the Chatichai period at 633.3 million baht per year, as compared to 86.3 million for Sarit, and 60.0 million baht in the case of Thanom-Praphat. But this comparison takes no account of the changing value of money, nor of the

Table 5.1 Total alleged wealth corruptly acquired by leading politicians (million baht)

	Sarit 1957-63	Thanom-Praphat 1964-73
1. Total alleged wealth corruptly acquired	2874	1000
2. Average per year	410.6	100.0
3. *(1) as % of capital expenditure in budget*	*30.2*	*1.7*
4. *(1) as % of annual government budget*	*4.2*	*0.5*
5. *(1) as % of GDP*	*0.67*	*0.0*

Note: This table shows the total of Sarit's legacy, most of which was acquired while he held office; and the total amount which Thanom-Praphat were *accused* of acquiring corruptly.

Table 5.2 Assets seized from leading politicians on grounds of corruption (million baht)

	Sarit 1957-63	Thanom Praphat 1964-73	Chatichai +ministers 1988-90	Chatichai alone 1988-90
1. Seized assets	604	600	1,900	284
2. Average per year	86.3	60.0	633.3	94.8
3. (1) as % of capital expenditure in budget	6.3	1.0	1.1	0.2
4. (1) as % of annual government budget	0.9	0.3	0.2	0.03
5. *(1) as % of GDP*	*0.14*	*0.05*	*0.04*	*0.01*

changing size of the economy and the government budget. When the corruption amount is expressed as a percentage of the government budget, then the Sarit period leads. Sarit's proven revenue from corruption amounted to 6.3 percent of the capital expenditure budget compared to 1.0 per cent by Thanom-Praphat and 1.1 per cent by Chatichai and his ministers. The total amount of Sarit's wealth, which appeared to have mostly been acquired during his term of office, amounted to 30.2 per cent of the capital expenditure budget across his years in office.

Similarly, political corruption as a percentage of GDP was at its highest in the Sarit period, at 0.14 per cent (0.67 per cent if we use his total wealth as the base). The rate in Thanom-Praphat was 0.05 per cent. and in the Chatichai period was 0.04 per cent. If we confine the corruption figure to the prime minister personally, the amount Chatichai was alleged to have acquired was only 0.01 per cent of the GDP.

These estimates indicate that if we look at the value of assets seized, the rate of corruption was highest in the Sarit period, and was higher under military-dominated governments than under the elected government of Chatichai.

The Sarit and Thanom-Praphat periods. Sarit's first will was written in February 1960. It revealed that his wealth during his early career as prime minister was modest. The will stated:

> 'After my death, I give all my cash and assets, rights and other claims which rightfully belong to me to Khun Ying Wijitra Thanarat alone, under the condition that she provides accommodation for Chettha Thanarat and Somchai Thanarat, each according to their status, and she gives Chettha Thanarat and Somchai Thanarat cash of one million baht each, totalling two million baht (that is if the total of amount of my cash is more than 10 million baht). My chicken farm and my other farms are to be divided equally between Chettha Thanarat and Somchai Thanarat for future operation. No other persons, whether or not a legitimate heir has any claim over any of my inheritance as specified in this will.'[27]

This will shows that around 1960 Sarit had wealth of around 10 million baht. Upon his death three years later he left over two billion baht in his inheritance. It is believed that the new economic development policies after 1960 opened up opportunities for Sarit and his men to amass wealth on a spectacular scale. Sarit himself manoeuvred to control key posts of government's decision-making in economic policy, namely the National Economic Development Board, the Board of Investment, and the Budget Bureau. These new public offices were directly under the Prime Minister's Office.

In 1959 Sarit moved the Budget Bureau to be under the Prime Minister's Office, and passed the Budgetary Procedures Act of 1959 which empowered the prime minister to transfer money from the central government budget to the secret funds of the Prime Minister's Office. The money was transferred into a bank account under the sole control of Sarit. When the government investigated the sources of Sarit wealth after his death, it was found that he had diverted 54 million baht of these funds for personal use.

Through control of the National Economic Development Board and the Board of Investment, Sarit gave companies owned by himself and his friends both investment privileges and monopolistic advantages. For instance, the Thai Saving Trust Company owned by Sarit had a monopoly of gold import. Several of Sarit's companies, such as the Bangkok Gunny Sack Company, were started with capital diverted from government coffers.[28]

Sarit also helped foreign firms to obtain operating licenses and monopolistic privileges, and was rewarded with a share in the ventures. For example, to assist foreign tin-mining companies, Sarit changed the mining laws. Subsequently he became a shareholder in several mining companies. Further, Sarit engineered a change in the land law, which previously provided for an upper limit on land ownership by individuals, so that he and his friends could own a large amount of land. He himself had land under his name totalling 22,000 rai, mostly in upcountry areas. Allegedly Sarit acquired much of this land by seizure without payment.[29]

The corruption practices by leading politicians in the Thanom-Praphat period (1962-73) were no different from those under Sarit. Praphat and Thanom were involved in setting up many companies which acted as government contractors and suppliers.[30] During the Thanom-Praphat period, there were several notorious corruption cases. It was alleged that aliens such as Indians and Chinese who wanted immigration visas had to pay at least 100,000 baht to General Praphat.[31] It was alleged that General Praphat allowed Nai Prasoet Pinthusophon to be the managing director of Borisat Samakki Khasat in return for 6,650 nominal shares. Later when this enterprise was transferred to the Bangkok Municipality, the Municipality paid General Praphat over 6 million baht for these shares which Praphat had received free.[32] There were many cases which alleged that General Praphat enabled businessmen to make use of the forest reserves without due consideration to the negative consequences on the society at large.[33] General Praphat was alleged to have received 50 million baht over 16 years as illegal bonuses from the Bangkok Electricity Authority.[34]

One of the most notorious cases involved the minister of agriculture. The minister and his wife received bribes from a private individual in return for a right to rent an area in the south from the Forestry Department for rubber plantation. The deal did not come off. The minister could not keep the promise but did not return the money. The briber asked for the money back. After many refusals he filed a court case against the minister and his wife, who had signed a receipt for the sums received. Because of the receipts, the court ruled that the minister and his wife were guilty.[35]

The Prem period. In the Prem period, we do not find cases involving the prime minister. However, cases involving other ministers and senior bureaucrats continued much as before.

A deputy agricultural minister was accused of trying to meddle with the bidding process in a fishery project.[36] An under-secretary of the Ministry of Defence was investigated by the CCC for being 'unusually rich'. He was found to have 70 million baht in his family bank accounts, and another 213 million baht worth of assets. He could not explain where this wealth had come from.[37]

Also during this period, officials in the Ministry of Education were charged over the construction of schools using sub-standard materials; an ex-judge and lawyers were accused of selling government land to private concerns for building a resort; eight police officers in Ubon were found to have looted over 88 million baht from the police budget;[38] officers of *tambon* councils in several provinces took money from the *tambon* funds;[39] police officers were investigated over drugs which disappeared after police seizure; police were accused of receiving protection money from gambling den owners; an official in Kasetsat University forged receipts, causing the university to lose over two million baht;[40] without informing the minister of finance, officials in Electricity Generating Authority of Thailand, the Petroleum Authority of Thailand and the Metropolitan Water Works Authority were engaged in multi-currency deals which caused debits in the accounts of the three offices of 983.1 million baht, 81.6 million baht and 145.8 million baht respectively;[41] and there were many cases of officials using government's equipment and property illegally.

The Chatichai period. The economic boom of the late 1980s changed the opportunities for political corruption. The cabinet had the power to decide on large infrastructure projects without recourse to debate in the parliament. Individual ministers also had the power to decide on large projects in each ministry without reference to cabinet or parliament—granting licences for new factories and financial firms; approving immigration quotas; granting concessions for logging or reforestation. The stock market boom after 1986 also created new opportunities for corruption. Firms were often anxious to secure a stock exchange listing. Entrepreneurs could reward favours with the gift of shares. Further, the trend towards privatization created other new opportunities.

As noted earlier, following the coup by the National Peace Keeping Council in February 1991, the prime minister, his aide and eight ministers were accused of being 'unusually wealthy'.

Their assets were seized. Among the seized assets were found a number of 'gift cheques' in the order of millions of baht given to the prime minister and some of the cabinet members. The details of the cheques were widely publicized. It was believed that the cheques were given by individuals and private companies in return for the granting of favours.

Large government projects involving billions of baht which were approved during the Chatichai period and were widely believed to be the source of corruption money for leading politicians included the elevated railway project (total project cost estimate of 42 billion baht) granted to Lavalin; the three million telephone line project (total project cost estimate of 150 billion baht) granted to a company in the Charoen Pokphand group; and several other large telecommunication projects. According to a leading businessman in the telecommunication industry, the commission fees involved in these projects were in the order of 3-5 per cent of the project cost.

The elevated railway and telephone line projects were approved in September and October of 1990 under the Chatichai government. But at the time of the NPKC coup, the final contracts had not been signed. The railway project was revoked at the end of 1991 because the new government and the concessionaires could not agree on certain technical matters. As for the three million telephone line project, the government led by Anand Panyarachun reviewed the project in 1992 and concluded that 'people feel that the decision regarding the said project involving a large sum of money and interest totalling hundreds of thousands of million baht, was not transparent enough, leading to suspicion as to the honesty of the selection'.[42] The Anand government split the project into two. The old concessionaire (Charoen Pokphand) retained the trimmed down project of two million telephone lines. The other one million lines were offered for fresh bidding, and the contract was granted to another private company.

After the Lavalin concession was revoked, the press reported that Lavalin had already paid kickbacks of up to one billion baht.[43] This might be an exaggeration as the project was not properly signed. At any rate the newspaper report acknowledged that this was only a rumour as there was no receipt to prove it.

Without receipts there is only circumstantial evidence to suggest the incidence of corruption among politicians. The existing anti-corruption laws inadequately cover corruption by politicians. The Office of Auditor General is only concerned with malpractice among bureaucrats in the use of government money. The Counter Corruption Commission can only investigate bureaucrats and politicians upon complaints. The CCC can investigate the prime minister and individual ministers only during their tenure of office. If complaints are lodged while they are in office, and later they leave office, the CCC can investigate them only within one year following. If the complaints are lodged after the minister has finished his term, the CCC has no right of investigation. MPs who do not hold a ministerial portfolio are not covered by the CCC, or any other counter-corruption organization. The CCC was set up by the executive to control corruption among bureaucrats. Thus its power to control the executive is limited.

In these circumstances, it is very difficult to pin down politicians on corruption charges. It is almost impossible to find hard information and expose it without being sued for libel. Thus the information on corruption used in most studies must be derived from official sources, such as the government seizure of assets following Sarit's death, after the fall of Thanom government, and following the NPKC coup of 1991.

The public is usually apprised of the extent of politicians' corruption only after the politicians have left office. However in the case of Chatichai and his cabinet, the public became aware of the alleged corruption during their term through widespread reports and speculation in the press. The formal charges of corruption were not laid against Chatichai's cabinet members until after they had been overthrown. At this point, the investigation of these charges inevitably acquired a political aspect. The investigation became a political tool which lacked clear and just criteria. For instance one of the ministers who was included in the 'unusually rich' group was later dropped from the list and was not investigated because he agreed to lead a new political party which was backed by members of the NPKC. Eventually four others of those accused with Chatichai were absolved of any guilt, and shortly after some turned up in the ranks of the NPKC-backed party. The incident highlighted the lack of any established machinery for monitoring and investigating corruption by ministers and politicians. The NPKC's investigation inevitably turned into a political weapon, and its findings were subsequently invalidated on those grounds.

The military, commission fees, and directorships

The Ministry of Defence is the only public office which keeps the details and the rationale of its expenditure secret from the parliament and from the public. The Ministry of Defence's operations and the purchase of arms are financed from the annual government budget, which in the end is the people's tax money. But security considerations have always been cited as the reason for not revealing the details of arms purchases and the use of 'secret funds', not even to parliament. According to former MPs who used to be members of the parliament's budget scrutinising committee, documents concerning the budget of the Ministry of Defence were very brief compared to those of other ministries, and often labelled as secret. Representatives of the Ministry would always refuse to answers questions posed by the budget scrutiny committee members on grounds of security. Similarly, the Office of Auditor General, which is empowered by law to investigate the accounts of government departments, faces all kinds of obstacles and objections in its attempts to look into the purchase of arms by the Ministry of Defence.

It is widely believed that top military officers in Thailand receive commission fees from arms purchases. A military officer has said: 'All this is only allegation. There is no corruption in the military. Arms purchases are between government and government. No one receives commission fees.'[44] However, an investigation by the *Asian Wall Street Journal* suggested rather different conclusions:

'Bangkok-based military analysts uniformly describe kickbacks and commissions from foreign weapons-manufacturing companies as commonplace. On a typical sale, Thai generals get 2% to 5% up front and as much as an additional 10% if the deal is signed, according to the analysts... The attraction of sales commissions also has led to redundant or excessive military weapons and supplies.'[45]

The military attaché of a foreign embassy who was involved in negotiations to sell arms to Thailand expressed his personal opinion that these negotiations had some unusual features. He felt surprised that the army's choice of weapons and suppliers often did not seem to be linked to 'military need' or 'suitability' of the type of weapons and equipment to local and regional conditions. Many very modern arms do not suit Thailand, and are not necessary. He suspected that the total amount of money involved in arms purchase was the most important consideration in the mind of the Thai military officers negotiating these purchases. According to him, 'arms purchase by the Thai military is not related to the need of the country, but is closely linked to how many top officers are about to retire, and need a lump of money for retirement or for other personal purposes'.[46]

We do not know the annual amounts involved in arms purchase because these are not disclosed for security reasons. But the amounts of some proposed individual purchase items are often revealed by rival arms dealers and reported in the press. These figures indicate the potential extent of the alleged commission fees. For instance, in 1991 the Ministry of Defence proposed a long-term purchase plan up to the year 2000 to the total amount of 53 billion baht.[47]

A leading person in Thai high society described the general features of commission payments:

'Assume that you contact me for a project, say building a road. The cost of the project is 100 million baht. I agree to the project. In return, you want to give me 10 million baht (10 per cent), which is from your own purse. It is not that this would reduce the project cost to 90 million baht. That is unacceptable. But the

10 million baht is *tam nam* [commission] or *sin nam jai* [gift of
good will]. People do this all over the world. There is nothing
wrong. I have seen this happening everywhere. My God... the
difference is only the method, the different techniques.
Therefore if all eyes are on this, damage will occur. Our country
will not progress as it should.'[48]

This individual argues that commission fees are a normal,
universal part of such large-scale transactions. The person also
suggests that the payment of such fees has no social dis-
advantages since the money comes from the businessman's own
pocket. This of course is naïve. The businessman will recover the
commission from the project cost. The payment of commission
inevitably results in some reduction in the quality, quantity or
value of the goods and services delivered against the contract.

Some military officers attempt to justify commissions on arms
purchases on similar grounds. They may also argue that the profit
from commissions is acceptable because it is used to strengthen
the army as an institution. A high-ranking military officer
interviewed on the matter of commission fees from arms
purchases said:

'It must be made clear that this company took the matter in their
own hands and gave a commission fee to this person of 10
million baht. Commission fees were paid. But the next thing,
what does the recipient do with this 10 million baht? Even if he
puts the money in his own pocket, I cannot conclude that he is
wrong. He may have to pay his subordinates, pay for charity
[*thot kathin*] or whatever. Some people take the 10 million baht
and give to their office. In fact to be a senior officer, the
government tries to help by providing some entertainment
allowances. But to be a commander in the army, we do not live
according to rules and regulations only. There is only this much
salary. Then a man's son goes into monkhood, another son gets
married. I do not have to help him because he has money. After
work we all go home. But soldiers are not like that... This is the
fact of military society. In private companies, there is no such

thing like this. They do not care. There is no need for closeness.
It is different.'[49]

This attitude gives legitimacy to corruption in the manner of
the old *gin muang* system. Senior military officers consider they
can legitimately receive commission fees because they use the
fees to sustain informal patronage ties which contribute to the
strength and culture of the army as an institution.

This kind of thinking among military officers has begun to
conflict with the attitude of the Thai public. In our study on
attitudes towards corruption among the Thai public (reported in
detail in chapter 5), we asked people how they would describe
the receiving of commission fees from arms purchases by military
officers. More than half (52.8 per cent) of 2,243 interviewees called
it 'corruption'. People believe the commission fee is corrupt,
because the damage falls upon the people who contribute the
taxation to pay for the high price of the arms.

The military on the boards of private firms. Unlike many
countries, Thailand's laws do not prohibit military officers from
sitting on the boards of directors of private companies. From our
study of the attitude of the Thai public towards corruption, we
found 5 per cent of the 2,243 sample respondents considered it
corruption if government officials, including military and police
officers, sit in the boards of directors of private firms while they
are still holding important government office. Among sub-
samples of businessmen, the urban poor and politicians, the
percentages having this opinion are slightly higher. Many more
people may not call the behaviour corruption, but consider it
'inappropriate', 'improper' and 'not right morally'. Our survey
suggests that some of the Thai public now consider the
appointment of senior government officials on the boards of
directors of private firms as an instance of corruption.

In as far as the military officers are concerned, this practice is
rampant. A number of high-ranking military officers are
members of the boards of directors of private firms. A study by
Teeranat shows the large numbers of high military officers on the
boards of golf course companies.[50]

Conclusion

In the late 1980s and early 1990s, corruption became a major topic of political debate, and an important weapon of political competition. The NPKC cited corruption as justification for overthrowing the elected government of Chatichai. The subsequent investigations helped to embroider the impression that corruption was extensive and inevitable under an elective regime.

This chapter set out to estimate the extent of corruption among regular government officials and top politicians, by expressing the quantifiable corruption money as percentages of the capital and material purchases portion of the annual budget, and as percentages of the GDP. The latter measurement helps us to see if corruption has actually expanded in line with the pace of economic development. Comparisons were made between the extent of corruption under different political regimes.

Corruption is obviously impossible to quantify with any degree of accuracy. The data which exist are partial, almost random in some cases, and politically biased in others. However, if we accept that the data are far from perfect, what can we still learn?

If we compare the amounts with which Chatichai's ministers were charged with similar amounts under the military regimes of Sarit and Thanom-Praphat, we find that the corruption of the military regimes was significantly larger. For each year in power, Sarit looted 0.14 per cent of the GDP compared to 0.05 per cent by Thanom-Praphat and 0.04 per cent by Chatichai and his ministers.

Obviously we have no guarantee that the amounts obtained by corruption which were taken as proven by courts and investigators were accurate. Yet there are other forms of evidence which corroborate the impression that corruption was higher under the dictatorial military regimes, and especially under Sarit. A high-ranking official in the Office of Auditor General said:

'Government under a dictatorial regime has the highest chance
to be most corrupt. This is because there is much concentration
of power. There is no need to share it with anyone else. In a
democratic regime, the rate of corruption is most likely lower
because it is more difficult. Corruption will more likely be
related to projects which are related to the growth of the
economy.'[51]

There are clearly some qualitative differences between the
forms of corruption practised by Sarit, Thanom, Praphat and
those practised by later elective politicians; and these qualitative
differences may add up to a quantitative shift as well.

Sarit was able to accumulate revenues from corruption by
many different methods. In particular, he was able to loot money
from the government's income stream, notably through the
lottery bureau and the military's secret funds. In addition he was
able to take a cut on many forms of expenditure, either by
forming shell companies to take a percentage from government
contracts, or by demanding kickbacks. Next he was able to
acquire assets at little or no cost by simple seizure. Through this
method he acquired enormous landholdings as well as corporate
shareholdings. Finally, he was also able to levy fees from
businessmen for manipulating the many rules and licensing
procedures. This varied range of opportunities for corruption
enabled Sarit to accumulate a corrupt income very rapidly. Over
just five years, his asset base grew from almost nothing to 2.8
billion baht, which would amount to around 80 billion baht at
today's value. At his death, Sarit's personal wealth was
equivalent to 42 per cent of the government budget.

Of the four forms of corruption practised by Sarit (income
diversion, cuts on expenditure, fees for services, asset seizures),
only two (fees for services, cuts on expenditures) accounted for
most of the corruption charges against Chatichai and his
ministers. The other forms have become progressively more
difficult because of the countervailing forces in a more democratic
system. Sarit looted the lottery bureau and secret funds with
impunity. None of the charges against Chatichai's men suggested
they had similar scope.

Under Chatichai, most of the *rumours* of corruption concerned kickbacks on the large expenditure projects. Most of the irregularities uncovered by the NPKC investigation, however, appear to have been more like fees for services rendered (help with a land deal, a licence, a reforestation contract).

Any attempt to compare the incidence of corruption by permanent officials over time is inevitably affected by the quality and compatibility of the data. In some periods, the monitoring authorities may have been more vigilant than others. However, some qualitative data may again give some indication of quantitative trends. First, the types of corruption seem to be remarkably similar across the period from the 1950s to the 1990s. Second, the distribution among the different ministries and departments shows more similarity than difference over time. These two qualitative indications suggest that bureaucratic corruption has been rather consistent over these four decades.

Our data show that the most common form of bureaucratic corruption throughout has been subtractions from the expenditure flows through collusion with contractors. Various case studies show that the rate of subtraction has tended to vary around 20-40 per cent. If we take the low end of that range and apply it to all forms of government expenditure on goods and services, then we have a rough estimate of the total value of bureaucratic corruption.

This method of estimation shows that the rate of corruption (as a per cent of GDP) increased in the Sarit period, peaked during Thanom-Praphat, and has since declined. It must be emphasized that these 'trends' are largely the product of the estimation method.

Data from the Office of Auditor General and the Counter Corruption Commission give some indication of the distribution across different ministries and departments. The annual reports of the Office of Auditor General show the amounts of money which had to be returned to the government by bureaucrats who engaged in corruption practices, cheating and misuse of government funds, both from the expenditure and revenue side. Misuse of funds and corruption occur in all ministries, all government offices. Excluding the Office of the Secretary General of the Parliament and the Office of the Royal Palace, the figures for 1990 showed that state enterprises topped the list followed by the Ministries of Defence, Industry, Agriculture, Communications, Education and Interior. As for the records of the Counter Corruption Commission, ministries with the highest cases of corruption investigated in 1990 were Interior, followed by Agriculture, Education, Public Health, Communications and Defence.

These official statistics tally with the Thai public's impression of the relative involvement of various government offices in corruption. In our survey of attitudes towards corruption we asked: when the word corruption is mentioned, what government office do you think of most? The answers from the sample survey of 2,243 people all over the country show the following:[52] the Police Department topped the list, followed by Defence, Interior, Communications, Land Department, Commerce, Agriculture, Customs Office, the Forestry Department, and Industry.

Notes

1.   Thak (1979: 172).

2.   Ukrist (1983: 174); Thak (1979: 335-8). Apart from 22,000 rai in the provinces, Sarit had another 300 plots in the capital.

3.   Wat, pseud., *Suek ching moradok* [Battle over the Inheritance], Bangkok: Mit Charoen Press, 1964, p.581, quoted in Thak (1979: 337).

4.   In the period of high growth in 1988-91 when land prices soared, there was a marked increase in reported cases involving evasion of land tax with cooperation from officers of the Land Department. See *Annual Reports of the Counter Corruption Commission, 1990, 1991, 1992*. Hereafter this series is referred to as *CCC Annual Report*.

5.   In the *CCC Annual Reports*, cases are classified according to the year they are resolved, not the year when they occurred.

6.   Chanuan (1976).

7.   *Siam Rath*, 22 April 1973 and 27 February 1974.

8.   *Siam Rath*, 3 and 5 February 1974; 18 August 1975.

9.   *Siam Rath*, 8 August 1971.

10. *Siam Rath*, 14 August 1973.

11. *Siam Rath*, October 1976.

12. *Siam Rath*, 5 June 1975.

13. *CCC Annual Report*, 1986.

14. *CCC Annual Report*, 1986.

15. *CCC Annual Report*, 1986.

16. *CCC Annual Report*, 1987.

17. *Siam Rath*, 10 August 1990, 10 November 1990.

18. *CCC Annual Report*, 1986.

19. *CCC Annual Report*, 1986.

20. *CCC Annual Report*, 1987.

21. *CCC Annual Report*, 1986.

22. *CCC Annual Report*, 1986.

23. *CCC Annual Report*, 1986.

24. *CCC Annual Report*, 1989.

25. *CCC Annual Report*, 1990.

26. These two departments fell within the Communications and Agriculture ministries respectively.

27. Cited in Ukrist (1983: 156).

28. Ukrist (1983).

29. Ukrist (1983).

30. Sungsidh (1983).

31. *Siam Rath*, 1 November 1973.

32. *Siam Rath*, 2 November, 1973.

33. *Siam Rath*, 10 November, 1973.

34. *Siam Rath*, 4 November, 1973.

35. See detailed reports in *Phim Thai* (1967).

36. *Bangkok Post*, 30 July 1987.

37. *Bangkok Post*, 12 November 1986; *CCC Annual Report*, 1986.

38. Office of Auditor General (1986: 76).

39. Office of Auditor General (1983: 60-62).

40. Office of Auditor General (1986: 72).

41. Office of Auditor General 1986: 161).

42. *Matichon*, 3 July 1992.

43. *Prachachat Thurakit*, 12-15 July 1992.

44. Quoted in *Siam Rath* Weekly, 12-18 July 1992.

45. Owens (1992).

46. Private interview with a military attaché, 1993.

47. Two per cent of this sum is 1.06 billion baht, five per cent is 2.65 billion baht and ten per cent is 5.3 billion baht.

48. *Phu Jatkan Raiwan*, 25 January 1993, p. 22.

49. Interview with a high-ranking army officer (*pan ek*), 1992.

50. Teeranat (1993).

51. An interview with a high-ranking official of the OAG on 2 June 1993.

52. See details of results of the attitude survey in chapter 5.

3
JAO PHO:
LOCAL INFLUENCE AND
DEMOCRACY

In recent years a number of influential provincial businessmen have been described in the press and in general conversation as *jao pho*, usually translated into English as 'godfather'.[1] The term conveys not only wealth and power but also an ability to operate above the law. Most are ethnic Chinese by origin and generally based in the provinces. They have wide business interests, covering both legitimate and criminal activities. They have groups of associates and followers. They move closely with powerful bureaucrats, policemen and military figures. They sit in positions of authority in local administration. They play a key role in parliamentary elections.

The phenomenon of the rich, local, ethnic Chinese merchant is hardly new. Bowring reported in the 1850s that the Chinese could be found 'penetrating every creek', working as traders, merchants and moneylenders.[2] Nor is their wish to operate above the law at all novel. In an incident reported in Samut Prakarn in 1927, a wealthy Chinese merchant, who was both a *kamnan* (local headman) and head of a Chinese secret society (*ang-yi*), shot dead a policeman and then attempted to gain immunity by bribing officials from the locality up to the minister of the interior himself.[3] In the 1950s it was said that local Chinese businessmen regularly tried to bribe or otherwise compromise senior local officials in order to have a free hand in their business dealings.[4]

Yet the prominence of the *jao pho* from the 1970s onwards is significantly different in two ways. First, they are relatively unguarded about the criminal aspect of their activities. Some boast about their ability to act above the law. Stories detailing their criminal activities are the stock-in-trade of the Thai press. Second, their role in local and especially national politics has become massive and obvious. Several *jao pho* have secured election to parliament. Some have risen to ministerial positions and one was nominated for the premiership. Others influence politics by financing candidates in local and general elections. It is also well-known that certain *jao pho* who are not themselves in parliament are nevertheless able to dictate the voting behaviour of several MPs who they have helped to secure election.

The active participation of *jao pho* in national politics has had an important impact on the power structure. They compete with the 'old élites' such as the military and bureaucracy for a share in the 'corruption money'. They manipulate the institutions of parliamentary democracy. They aim to use the resulting power to maintain their status 'above the law' in order to further their business interests, both legal and illegal. The emergence of the *jao pho* to such a position of importance in national politics raises several questions. Is this a passing phase of Thailand's economic and democratic growth? Or is it the first stage in the emergence of a structure of political boss-ism or gang-ism on par with the Italian Mafia or the political structure of some Latin American countries? What are the forces opposed to the *jao pho* and how can their strength be developed?

This chapter discusses the rise of the provincial *jao pho* as a new 'player' in the Thai socio-economic and power structure during the period of high economic growth and democratic expansion, and analyses their role in political corruption and the development of democratic politics. The chapter begins with some explanation of the term *jao pho*, presents some case studies from five upcountry provinces, and then analyses the phenomenon of the modern *jao pho* in terms of their economic background, their sources of informal influence, their role in local politics, and their penetration of national politics. The chapter ends with discussion of the regional distribution of the *jao pho*, and of the impact of their rise on the development of Thailand's democracy.

What is a *jao pho*?

The term *jao pho* (and also *jao mae* in the case of a woman) is traditionally used to refer to a god (goddess), or to a spirit residing in a place. This spirit could belong to a dead person. It has been a common practice for people to set up shrines to appease the spirits of those who met untimely deaths such as through accident or suicide. Some of these shrines earn a reputation of sanctity or supernatural power, generally as a result of reports by people who prayed at the shrine and were granted their wishes, or who in some other way experienced some unusual event at the place. In time such shrines earn the reputation for being the residence of a certain *jao pho/mae*.

In the context of present-day Thailand the term is used to refer to an influential person who can use his wealth and informal power (through patronage, bribery, violence or other means) to put himself above the law and to provide extra-legal protection for others. According to the Thai dictionary, *Chabap ratcha-banditsathan*, the term *jao pho* refers to those important people with *itthiphon* (influence) in the locality. The term may have been derived from the traditional use of *jao pho*, by associating the ability to be above the law with the extraordinary, supernatural power of a traditional *jao pho* shrine. According to a journalist, the modern usage of the term *jao pho* may have been invented to translate the title of the film 'The Godfather'. Certainly since the showing of the film, the term *jao pho* has been popularly used to describe rich, influential persons who successfully flaunt the law.[5] The term has tended to supplant the more formal description of 'men of influence' (*phu mi itthiphon*) or the more expressive 'dark influences' (*itthiphon meut*) which enjoyed a vogue in the mid-1980s.

The term *jao pho* is sometimes used in conjunction with *nak leng*, a traditional term now used to refer to a tough man, a rowdy and aggressive type, who is likely to be a crook and have a tendency to be violent. In the past, the term *nak leng* was used to describe a tough but generous and gentlemanly fellow whose basic motive was to protect his village against the abuse of outsiders and bandits.[6] The term acquired connotations of rebelliousness and honour. Traditional stories tell of *nak leng* who helped people in the locality by any means possible, even to the extent of robbing from the rich to aid the local poor. They existed in areas where the mechanism of official administration was remote, and often they opposed attempts to make the administration more effective.

The modern usage of *nak leng* contains a mixture of negative and positive connotations. It may describe men who are tough, independent and who are prepared to use their command of brute force to assist underdogs in the face of the brutality of other rogues or government officials. *Nak leng* of this type are seen as generous, loyal and true to a certain moral code. Yet at the same time it can also be applied to a simple gangster, who wields brute force for personal gain and with criminal intent.

The terms *jao pho* and *nak leng* clearly occupy some of the same cultural space. In the same way that *nak leng* in the past existed because of the inefficiency of central administration in maintaining law and order and dispensing justice, *jao pho* in present-day Thailand exist and flourish because of the laxity of the central administration and because of the susceptibility of civil officials and military officers to corruption.

However, in many crucial respects the two terms, *jao pho* and *nak leng*, are significantly different. A *nak leng* is a simple tough who may have his admirable side but may equally be a simple criminal. A *jao pho* is a leader. A *nak leng* may flaunt the law but he is subject to it. A *jao pho* generally operates (or aims to operate) above the law. *Jao pho* may possess the positive traits or characteristics of *nak leng*, namely their generosity, loyalty and moral code (of being true to their word). But most *jao pho* also accumulate wealth through illegal means, often behave like gangsters, and frequently hire simple *nak leng* as their assistants. Furthermore, while *nak leng* tend to be local figures, *jao pho* in the present-day context are often able to extend their power across several provinces and to carve out a role in the politics of the nation. Sombat Chantornvong defines *jao pho* as those wealthy men who have influence over high officials, and who use their informal influence to act above the law.[7] Implicit in his argument is that *jao pho* tend to be agents of violence.

In this chapter we are concerned with the provincial variant of *jao pho* and their followers. They come from all regions of the country. Their origins and activities are immensely diverse. Our main concern however is with *jao pho* or *phu mi itthiphon* (men with influence) who have become important in local and national politics either as organizers of canvassers, or as supporters of certain politicians and political parties, or as politicians themselves. It also treats of those who once had the reputation as *jao pho* but who have 'cleansed' themselves by being elected as MPs, or by being appointed into official positions. Thus *jao pho* in our discussion is slightly different from that defined by Sombat Chantornvong, who stressed the tendency to act 'above the law' and deploy violence. Our *jao pho* will be broader. The term will cover influential provincial businessmen who may accumulate wealth by legal or illegal means, but who are rich enough and possess sufficient *itthiphon* that they may sometimes flaunt the law, or protect others from it.

While the term *jao pho* suggests a tendency to act 'above the law', not all those identified as *jao pho* engage in criminal activities and use violence. Of course, as the case studies below indicate, some of the major *jao pho* have acted in the gangster tradition replete with gambling, protection rackets, smuggling and gunplay. But others have merely used their considerable *itthiphon* to take advantage of the weakness of local administration, to prosecute their business and political careers in ways which would fall foul of a stricter juridical regime. They have made friends with the forces of law and order and often ensured that these forces are either in their pay or in their debt. From this vantage point they may not actually act 'against' the law, but often are able effectively to act as if 'above' it.

Case studies: nine lives of *jao pho*

These five case studies[8] focus on nine *jao pho* who have spread their influence beyond a single town or province and who have had an impact on national politics. They include some of the most famous of all the *jao pho*, but certainly not all of those who have exerted such extensive influence. First is the case of Kamnan Bo, perhaps the nation's single most famous *jao pho* (a description he himself denies), who began his career as a fisherman in the eastern coastal port of Chonburi, who became a major force in business and local politics, and who now has two sons sitting on the benches of parliament. This case study also traces the careers of Kamnan Bo's predecessors in Chonburi, in order to present a historical perspective running from the Thanom-Praphat military dictatorship through to the democratic period of the late 1980s and early 1990s. The second case is the story of a *jao pho* who began as a bicycle repairman, who rose to be the financial backer of up to 25 MPs, who died in a spectacular gangland killing, and whose funeral was attended by the minister of the interior. Third is the case of a central region *jao pho* who started as a grocery delivery boy, who became the biggest political broker of the northeastern region, and who to date has survived at least four gang-style 'hits'. The fourth case concerns a family of three *jao pho* in Petchburi, whose ancestors began as provincial officials, who later were said to have diversified into several criminal and highly lucrative sidelines, and who all three sat on the benches of parliament in the 1980s. The last is about a northern *jao pho* who rose from logging and export of tobacco to ministerial office and who was denied the premiership on grounds of suspected involvement in drug trafficking.

Sia[9] Jiew and Kamnan Bo of Chonburi. Chonburi used to be a sleepy fishing port and resort town before a highway was built covering the 87 kms to Bangkok in 1975. Since then Chonburi has become one of the most prosperous, most lively and most violent of all Thailand's provincial centres. The town developed on the basis of several businesses: trade in new agricultural crops, tourism and smuggling. The town lies close to the port used for loading tapioca pellets bound for Europe. Just down the road are the major tourist centres of Bang Saen (for local tourists) and Pattaya (for foreigners). A little way along the coast lie Cambodia and Vietnam. And only a few kilometres from Chonburi lies Laem Chabang, site of a major port and industrial zone under the eastern seaboard project, the country's largest single venture in industrial development.

Besides legitimate business, Chonburi has a thriving underworld. As a small seaport close to Bangkok, Chonburi has always been convenient for the smuggling trade. Fishing boats have been discovered carrying imported cigarettes, liquor, electrical goods, drugs, minerals and arms. Driven by demand from local wealth and from tourism, the area developed a reputation for gambling dens, underground lotteries, and prostitution. The combination of legitimate and illegitimate ways of making money has proved the foundation for a rich and turbulent local history.

In the 1960s the prominent *jao pho* was Kiang Jungprasert, or Long Ju Kiang[10], who was said to have risen to influence through association with General Praphat Charusathian (army field marshal; army commander 1963-1972, deputy prime minister 1966-1973), and with Sudsai Thephasdin, a key man in Internal Security Operations Command (ISOC)[11], the army's counter-insurgency unit. Kiang obtained from the government the concession to a lucrative mine in the province of Chonburi, and was said to have secured an effective monopoly of saw mills, rice mills, plantations, mining and a whole host of other activities.

Kiang died in a car accident, and his two sons inherited his empire. Both by this time had acquired influential posts in the local administration. One of them was a *phuyaiban* (village head) in Ban Bung (a sub-district of Chonburi). The other had been a deputy district officer in Mae Hong Son province in the north. After Kiang's death, one of his erstwhile lieutenants, Sia Jiew, declared a gang war against the sons. One of the sons announced that he intended to be the only *jao pho* in Chonburi. Shortly after, both he and his brother were gunned down in separate incidents. The gunman who killed one of the sons was known to be an associate of Sia Jiew.[12]

Sia Jiew (Jumpol Sukparangsi) began his career as a supervisor of bus conductors, and later ran a pig slaughtering business. After the death of Kiang and the elimination of the sons, Sia Jiew took over as the towns's leading *jao pho* and expanded into saw milling, rice milling, petrol stations, hotels and whisky wholesaling. In the mid-1970s he built up his connections by working as *hua kanaen* (vote bank) for two local politicians, Thamanoon Thienngeon and Boonchu Rojanasathian. Sia Jiew used his *barami* (powerful position) to help Boonchu, a relatively unknown politician, to succeed against Siri Siriyothin, a prominent old-time local politician (*jao thin*) and army man.[13] In an interview with a newspaper, Sia Jiew explained why he helped Boonchu. Sia Jiew himself was uneducated whereas Boonchu was highly educated and had risen to the top management rank in the Bangkok Bank. Moreover, Boonchu was a Chonburi man. Sia Jiew might also have added that Boonchu was, like him, a second-generation ethnic Chinese. By helping to secure Boonchu's election, Sia Jiew was helping promote one of the most dazzling scions of Chonburi's Chinese community, and at the same time building a powerful connection in the heady political realms of Bangkok.

Sia Jiew had three close aides and friends who each looked after important sections of his business empire. Kamnan Bo looked after soil and gravel transport, construction contracting and road building. Sia Lin (U'thai Hirisatja) took care of fish and shrimp farming. Sia Thong looked after the whisky agency. Sia Jiew personally controlled the hotels and shopping centres.[14] All of the group had developed wide connections within the locality.

Sia Jiew built up his connections with big men in the army, and he was a devout supporter of the Village Scouts, a local support group organizied by the Border Patrol Police to combat communist influence. Sia Lin's wife was president of the Village Scouts in the eastern region. Sia Jiew gave large donations for charity, which raised his status in the community. His son Paan looked after the delicate business of enforcement. It was said that Paan used his *itthiphon* and protection from an important army man to carry out many illegal activities. He had reportedly ordered the gunning down of more than 10 people who were in the opposite camp.

The rivalry between the groups of Sia Jiew and the late Kiang was not confined to business and gunplay. From the mid-1970s, it also extended to parliamentary elections. Sia Jiew sided with

Kitsangkom (Social Action), the party of Boonchu, Kukrit and later Montri Pongpanich. The followers of Kiang (Phu Yai Lee, Phu Yai Ieak) supported the opposing Gaew Na (Progressive) party and Ekaparp (Solidarity) party led by Uthai Pimchaichon.

In the early 1980s the conflicts became very acute. In 1981, Sia Jiew died after his car was attacked on a major highway and blown away by a rocket launcher and automatic gunfire. His son was killed in 1984, allegedly at the cost of half a million baht provided by a consortium of pig merchants, mining entrepreneurs and other rising *jao pho*. The police failed to find the culprits. After Sia Jiew's death, one of his lieutenants, Kamnan Bo, took over his empire and expanded it on a scale that made the efforts of his predecessors seem very small-time.

Kamnan Bo (Somchai Kunpluem) was born in 1937 in a family of eight children in a fishing village close to Chonburi. His parents ran the village grocery store. He received four years of elementary education and started his working career as a bus conductor. He was elected *kamnan* in 1979 and was known thereafter as Kamnan Bo.

When he was 17 he worked as a wage labourer on the fishing boats, and in 1962 he married an elder sister of Nikom Saencharoen, who later became an MP of the Kitsangkom Party and a deputy minister of communications. By the time he was 30 (1967) he managed to acquire his own fishing boat. The turning point came in 1971-2 when he seized an opportunity to fish in Cambodian waters. With colleagues who in total owned around 15 boats, he set up an unofficial company and was able to obtain a licence from the Cambodian government in return for a fee of 100,000 baht per year. The company was not officially registered in Thailand, and the group did not inform anyone when they went to Cambodia.

The venture was very lucrative. Each trip netted hundreds of thousand of baht, several times the annual licence fee. As the organizer, Kamnan Bo obtained 20 per cent cut of the proceeds of all other boats. He also made money by trading United States dollars between the American base in Sattahip and the black market in Cambodia. The fishing ventures lasted two years, after which he had to quit because of problems with Cambodian officials, and because of the civil war. The venture had totally changed his economic status and now he began to invest widely in other businesses. His timing was perfect for Chonburi's economic take-off.

The quick money was in construction. Bo started up new ventures in transporting soil and gravel for road building and landfill, and in construction contracting for road building. Smuggling contraband goods along the east coast increased in this period.[15] Bo was alleged to have extensive links with *jao pho* involved in gambling dens in Bangkok who facilitated the transportation of smuggled goods at the Bangkok end.[16]

He put his profits into building a chain of massage parlours and hotels. He secured the sole distributorship for local whisky (Maekhong, Hongthong) throughout Chonburi—a highly profitable monopoly. With all these activities his business empire expanded very quickly. When the real estate boom hit Chonburi in the mid-1980s, Bo used his local knowledge and influence to become the biggest real estate dealer in the region. By 1987 he owned all the land along both sides of road number 331 linking Chachoengsao and Sattahip. In the municipality of Sriracha he forged links with the biggest real estate dealer, the Menglee-Chaimongkol group. He also acquired many thousands of *rai* of land in Bang Saen.

As tourism began to boom in the 1980s, Kamnan Bo invested in resorts, hotels and shopping complexes in Bang Saen, Pattaya and Chonburi, including the Bang Saen Plaza and the Happy World entertainment complex. From 1986, Bo carried out a major redevelopment of Bang Saen, resettling slums away from the beach areas, and vastly increasing its attraction as a tourist centre. Bo then built bungalows and rented them out to private individuals. These areas had originally been classified as public land and so were unavailable to private developers, but by this time Bo was in a position to sort out such minor problems. He also succeeded in persuading the Tourist Authority of Thailand to lease him a large hotel in Bang Saen for fifteen years. He turned the moribund hotel into a highly profitable venture. He became the sole magnate of the highly popular Bang Saen resort.

In the mid-1980s, the local real estate market received another boost. The cabinet approved the eastern seaboard development plan in 1981 and finally began construction on the massive project in 1987. The prospect that the project would bring a large increase in population and secondary businesses to the whole surrounding area sparked off a land boom. Speculators bought up land around Laem Chabang, raising the land price by more than 10 times in a few years. Bo did not invest in the industrial ventures of the eastern seaboard, as he did not have the expertise and the skill of modern management. He confined his ventures to ancillary activities like resorts, housing and land speculation.

As Bo's business expanded, so also did his political connections and his control of public office. He was elected the *phuyaiban* (village headman) of Tambon Saensuk (Bang Saen) in 1967 at the start of his career as a fishing entrepreneur. He was chosen as *kamnan* in 1979 when his business career was really taking off. In 1988 he resigned from being *kamnan* to make it easier for him to play an active role in support of Kitsangkom (Social Action) in the national elections. In 1989 Tambon Saensuk was raised to a municipality and Bo was elected mayor unopposed.

In the locality he presents himself as a generous man. He explains that since he makes so much money and cannot take it with him to his grave, it is only natural that he should give generously. Anyone in the community can bring their problems to him. He also gives generously for public projects. He says a selfish person does no good to the society. He claims to spend more than 10 million baht a year on public projects such as building roads, installing sewage systems, constructing and repairing Chinese temples. In addition he donates money to other government projects. He likes to tell newspaper interviewers: 'I only give'.

Bo is very proud of the relocation of slums from the beach of Bang Saen. He was able to persuade all the slum dwellers to move to a site of eight *rai* he himself bought for one million baht. Now about 100 families live in this land on the condition that they cannot sublease their plot if they move out. Land which is vacated is taken over by the village committee and planted with trees so that the village, called Chokdee or Lucky Village, is gradually becoming greener. The rent is set at twenty baht per month, but Bo claims that he has never collected any.

Kamnan Bo's investment in public works and projects like the slum relocations have enhanced his popularity as well as assisting in the long-run success of his other more directly productive investments in housing and resort facilities in Bang Saen. His generosity with the villagers enabled him to be accepted and respected in the community. All this makes him a valuable *hua kanaen* or vote bank for political parties. And finally in turn his connections with politicians and with other influential officials enable him to bring more large public projects into the locality, adding further to his status as a generous and effective local leader.

Bo also built up his followers and supporters through his business dealings. He has not ventured into farming or mining, largely to avoid conflict with powerful established interests. Big agricultural ventures such as cassava and sugarcane were the province of Damrong Singtothong (Hia Sui), president of the Sugar Cane Plantation Association of Chonburi and many times an MP. Mining was controlled by another big local businessman, Supakit Prasomsap (Kamnan Lee). Bo carefully built his business empire in a way which did not tread on the toes of such established local entrepreneurs.

Like other well-established *jao pho*, Kamnan Bo let his sons and associates manage most of his businesses. He himself took personal control of the real estate business in partnership with an associate, Nawamit Mahanakhon. Somchai, his eldest son, manages the hotels and resort businesses including S.S. Villa, Hotel Bang Saen, and Bang Saen Beach Resort (the TAT hotel). Various other businesses are controlled by a wide ring of associates. By allowing his men to run most of the businesses on his behalf, and by developing mutually profitable alliances with other major local entrepreneurs, Bo has developed a wide network of friends and dependents. For instance, Bo works closely with Somboon Tiemratananon (Tiem), who supplies fresh foods to the hotels, resorts and entertainment complexes in Bo's empire. The business relationship runs largely on mutual trust without recourse to documents which might not always be convenient. As long as they run the businesses to the satisfaction of Bo, the associates are open to make money for themselves in the process. By this means, Bo has collected a lot of followers many of whom are considered by some to be tough *nak leng.*

Chonburi has the highest crime rate in the country, and many incidents of murder and violence have all the marks of gang warfare between influential interests. However, in contrast to Kiang and Sia Jiew, Bo is not directly identified with acts of gang violence. In 1989, Sia Huad, a Chonburi *jao pho* and a rival to Bo, was shot dead after a car chase and gun battle along the province's main roads. Sia Huad had recently outbid Bo to control a large trade centre project in Chonburi town. Bo dismissed suggestions that he was linked with the killings and simply said that 'in Chonburi, bad guys must die'.[17] Four years later in March 1993 in what appeared to be a revenge killing, three notorious local *nak leng* who were said by some to be associates of Bo and who included a man accused of the Sia Huad killing, were found shot dead beside a road in Saraburi. Bo denied any connection with the three.[18] Yet Bo also refers to himself as a 'semi-businessman semi-gangster' (*kung nak thurakit kung nak leng*).[19]

Bo's large network of contacts built through business and through social activity comes into its own at election time. Bo has been involved in bringing out the local vote on behalf of favoured candidates since 1975. In each election from 1975 to 1992, he has been instrumental in the success of two to four candidates.

Following his early association with Boonchu, much of Bo's electoral support has gone to the Kitsangkom (Social Action Party). But Bo claims he is indifferent to party loyalty and explains that he supports candidates simply because of personal relations, because they are 'one of us' (*pen phakphuak diew kan*). Many of his protégés are relatives and associates. Nikom is his brother-in-law and Charun is also a relative. Wittaya and Sonthaya are his own sons. In other cases, Bo's assistance was traded for reciprocal gain. Sompong whom Bo helped in 1986 had powerful connections in the military, the police, and the world of banking. Sompong's brother, Sawat, became director of the police in 1992. Sompong himself was married into the Tejaphaibun banking family, and Sompong had reportedly smoothed the way for Bo to get financing for his projects from the Srinakorn Bank.[20]

Kamnan Bo helped candidates through his network of informal influence with *kamnan*, *phuyaiban*, businessmen and local officials who were able to influence voters to attend the poll and vote on behalf of Bo's candidates. He also helped by more extreme methods. In an interview he revealed that he used his influence to vote on behalf of eligible voters who did not turn up

Successful electoral candidates supported by Kamnan Bo

Date	Member of Parliament	Party
1975	Boonchu Rojanasathian	Kitsangkom
	Damrong Singtothong	Santichon
1976	Boonchu Rojanasathian	Kitsangkom
	Siri Siriyothin	Chart Thai
1977	Prayote Nuengjamnong	Independent
	Damrong Singtothong	Kitsangkom
	Siri Siriyothin	Chart Thai
1983	Prayote Nuengjamnon	Chart Prachathipatai
	Damrong Singtothong	Kitsangkom
	Nikom Saencharoen	Kitsangkom
	Charun Ngampichet	Kitsangkom
1986	Sompong Amornwiwat	Chart Prachathipatai
	Charun Ngampichet	Kitsangkom
	Nikom Saencharoen	Kitsangkom
1988	Nikom Saencharoen	Kitsangkom
	Tirdtham Amralikhit	Kitsangkom
	Charun Ngampichet	Kitsangkom
	Thavorn Triratnarong	Kitsangkom
1992 (September)	Wittaya Kunpluem	Chart Pattana
	Sonthaya Kunpluem	Chart Pattana

Source: Viengrat (1989).

at the polling booth. His men would keep going into the polling booth repeatedly using their own identity cards, and the poll officials were persuaded to cooperate and pretend not to know what was going on. He confessed that the large turnout figures in Chonburi polls may have been the result of his subordinates' over-enthusiasm.[21]

Sia Yae of Angthong.[22] Sia Yae (Somchai Rerkvararak) was born in 1936 to an overseas Chinese father and a Chinese-Thai mother. His father was a goldsmith in Angthong, a paddy-growing area in the central region. Sia Yae had only four years of elementary education and in his young days he earned a living from bicycle repairs. The turning point of his life came after his father's death in the mid-1950s when he opened a gambling den. With the income from the gambling den, he expanded his bicycle repair business into a metal workshop producing iron gates and windows, and later extended into trading in construction materials. As he became more successful he began making contacts with local officials and politicians. He was able to secure government contracts to supply materials for construction of schools and roads in the province, and gradually set himself up as a construction contractor. His contacts with local officialdom drew even closer in 1966 when at the age of thirty he married a woman who was related both to an influential police officer who later rose to a high position in the police department and also to a major dealer in arms for the Thai military.

In about the early 1960s he began moving into the timber trade as part of his construction materials business. In the mid-1970s, when there was a shortage of timber in the market, Sia Yae moved into the lumber processing business and rented a small sawmill in the neighbouring province of Ayutthaya. Later he bought the mill in Ayutthaya and expanded by buying more sawmills in Sakon Nakhon, Chaiyaphum and Loei in the northeastern region. Next he used his connections with police and army officers to obtain logging concession in many provinces in the central and northeast regions. He finally spread his construction business into the northeast (Chaiyaphum) and also invested in a shrimp farm in Samut Sakhon, and in a transportation company.

Sia Yae would not have been able to build up his empire, especially the lucrative logging concessions, without political connections and he devoted considerable attention to this aspect of his business. Beginning in Angthong he sponsored local politicians including *phuyaiban*, *kamnan*, and members of the provincial and municipal councils (*so jo* and *samachik thesaban*). He himself became president of the Angthong Chamber of Commerce. Because of his limited education he was unable to stand as a parliamentary candidate but he became instead the chief financial backer of candidates in Angthong. Gradually he widened his financial support to include local politicians in Chaiyaphum where he had his sawmills, and to members of parliament in other provinces where he had business interests. He donated to the Chart Thai Party, which led him to be appointed to the party executive committee. He was allowed to choose the party candidates in provinces where he was influential. In 1986 he resigned from his official position in the party following conflict with the party's secretary general. He continued to support MPs from the Chart Thai Party but also diversified his support to other parties. At the time of his death in 1989, it was reported that at least 10 and possibly as many as 25 MPs were supported by Sia Yae.

As Sia Yae expanded his business empire and developed his political connections, he created enemies along the way. In 1983 five gunmen with M-16s sprayed his car with bullets but Sia Yae survived. Six months later a former Angthong MP who was a rival of Sia Yae was attacked by six men and severely crippled. One of the gunmen later described the assault as a revenge for the attempt on Sia Yae's life. In February 1988 another rival of Sia Yae was killed by a gunman in Bangkok. Five months later, there was another attempt on Sia Yae's life. He and his wife were both injured but again survived. He swore revenge from his hospital bed. A week after he was released from hospital, a son of his rival in Angthong was killed in a hail of bullets. A *phuyaiban* from Ayutthaya who had been elected with Sia Yae's support was arrested for his role in the killing.

Sia Yae eventually lost his life in 1989. As he was leaving the court house in the northeastern provincial capital of Korat, a modified claymore mine was detonated by remote control killing Sia Yae and several of his companions. The assassination method suggested some expertise with explosives which is usually acquired in the military.

For someone who had died in a fashion worthy of the most melodramatic gangster movie, his funeral was truly a star-studded affair. The guest of honour was the minister of interior along with several other ministers and MPs.

Sia Yae started out as the son of a Chinese immigrant, began his business career as a bicycle repairman, made his first pile by managing a gambling den, married the relation of a police officer, rose from being a nobody in a sleepy provincial town of Angthong to become a manipulator at the highest level of government, gave all three of his sons the college education he never had, died in a spectacular assassination on the steps of a court house, and was mourned by some of the leading politicians in the land.

Sia L— of Khon Kaen. Sia L— was born in 1934 in Nakhon Ratchasima (Korat). Both of his parents had migrated from mainland China. He said his family was poor. He had four years of elementary schooling in a Chinese school. When he left school he had to help the family by selling noodles, until a grocery store owner in Khon Kaen offered him a job as an all-round shop assistant and delivery boy. He was good at the job and after four or five years he was promoted to look after buying supplies. He travelled a lot and acquired a good knowledge of the surrounding areas in the northeast. With his promotion he received 700 baht a month and he began studying Chinese and accountancy by correspondence. After his study he was promoted to the position of accountant. When he was 28 he left the shop and started his own business.

With the help of a friend, he borrowed several thousand baht from a bank and began buying and selling cash crops around Khon Kaen. Once he had some capital, he also acted as a moneylender, advancing the villagers cash and seed in return for a lien on the crop. Next he invested in processing the crops. He set up a flour mill, a cassava processing plant and a rice mill. Finally he extended into a crop wholesaling business and into crop exporting.

When he was around 40 (in the early 1970s) he had the capital to expand into areas which required higher investment but also yielded higher return. He got into logging, and from there into commercial forestry. He invested more than 50 million baht in eucalyptus and bamboo plantations on 4,000 *rai* of land bordering Khon Kaen and Korat. He also had a granite mining firm in Loei. Finally he became involved in the lucrative area of real estate and urban development in Khon Kaen. His business extended to hotels, real estate, housing development, shopping complexes and condominiums. He managed this sprawling empire with the help of his wife, his brother and other close aides. He sent his son for schooling in the United Kingdom and on his return the son helped to manage the business empire.

Sia L— liked gambling. As he developed his legitimate business from his base in Khon Kaen across wide areas of the northeast, he is also said to have developed an underground lottery. He is alleged to have begun to deposit large sums of money from the lottery operations in one of the prominent banks. It was large enough to make him an important customer of a leading banker who later formed a political party to contest in elections. Sia L— became an important supporter of the party in the northeast.[23] His gambling and the lucrative underground lottery in many parts of the region more than anything else earned him the legendary title as the '*jao pho* of the northeast' (*jao pho daen Isan*). As he became richer he spent more of his time in Bangkok and became a frequent client of Bangkok's big-time gambling bosses, who have extensive links with high military and police officers.[24] He tried to start a club himself in Bangkok but was not successful because of police harassment. He then was alleged to have leased a gambling den. The venture was profitable for the two partners until Sia L— decided to switch patrons and began operating another den for a rival. Shortly after this he became the target of an attack by a gunman, which he narrowly survived. This was not the first such instance: he had survived an earlier assault in 1983. Meanwhile in Khon Kaen, two of his rivals, Sia Yoo and Sia Lek, were killed in gangland wars.[25]

Because of his underworld activities and the gang conflicts which they involved, Sia L— needed protection and hence he cultivated friendships with military men and high officials. In his own words, 'I was a poor man before and did not have much education. Thus whatever I do I have to rely on friends and connections in politics'.[26] He said in an interview with a newspaper that he was friendly with many high-ranking military officers, especially General Sunthorn Kongsompong. He was so close to Sunthorn that he regularly had drinks with him.[27] He also cultivated his relationship with General Chavalit Yongchaiyuth by assisting with Chavalit's *Isan Khiew* (Green Northeast) project. With these connections Sia L— received more than just protection. It is alleged that he was helped to expand into logging and trading across the borders into Burma and Laos.[28] On 15 April 1990, a gunman tried to kill Sia L— in Bangkok but he again survived. In hospital he received flowers and sympathy from, among others, Sunthorn Kongsompong, by now the Army Supreme Commander; Klaeo Thanikul, the most notorious gambling magnate in Bangkok; and the MP for Surin.[29] The secretary general of the Democrat Party, also visited him on grounds of being an old friend.[30]

By the mid-1980s, Sia L—'s influence was also important in parliamentary elections. At the 1986 election, five successful candidates under Boonchu's Community Action Party (Kitprachakom) were reportedly financed by Sia L—. In 1987, Sia L— had an opportunity to show his informal influence over these MPs.

The Community Action Party belonged to the opposition to prime minister Prem. In April 1987, the opposition mounted a no-confidence motion against the government. General Sunthorn Kongsompong lobbied Sia L— to persuade the MPs under his influence not to vote with the opposition. Sunthorn himself went to fetch Sia L— from his Khon Kaen home to come to Bangkok to talk to all the MPs in his camp. The result was that the five MPs withdrew their name from the motion and the motion failed.[31]

The incident seemed to persuade Sia L— that he should sponsor parties with strong military links. He broke with Boonchu and took his cadre of MPs into the Rassadorn Party of former deputy premier General Tienchai Sirisamphan. In the election of 1988, Sia L— distributed his eggs in several baskets and gave support to candidates of different parties including Rassadorn (General Tienchai), Chart Thai (Generals Pramarn and Chatichai), Puangchon Chao Thai (General Arthit) and Kitsangkom. He reportedly financed about ten candidates but only two were elected. In the September 1992 election Sia L— supported the Kwamwangmai party (General Chavalit) and was appointed as coordinator of the party's candidates for the northeastern region. He boasted that his party should net at least 50 MPs in the northeast alone. The party eventually won 40 seats with 31 of this total in the northeast. Sia L— subsequently paid a visit to Bangkok and summoned 'his' MPs to appear in audience before him.

The A— family of Petchburi. Petchburi is notorious as the gunman capital of Thailand. In terms of crime statistics it ranks third (behind Chonburi and Nakhon Sithammarat), and less than 50 per cent of reported crimes lead to convictions. Murders are common and the province is reputed to have the highest concentration of guns for hire. At one time it was said that anyone wanting to have s meone eliminated would not be disappointed if he contracted a Petchburi gunman.[32] It was also alleged that during the 1970s and the 1980s at least a hundred novice gunmen associated with one of the leading *jao pho* had been liquidated by the police.[33]

Petchburi's violent reputation stems from the business opportunities offered by the province's location. Petchburi is a coastal province 150 kms from Bangkok on the southern peninsula. Its fishing port is an ideal location for coastal smuggling. Its forested hills contain several tracks leading into Burma. The province's *jao pho* have many opportunities for smuggling imported goods destined for Bangkok, for bringing illegal timber from Burma, and for trading in other illegal items.

Petchburi town acquired a thriving underworld famous for gambling and underground lotteries.

Petchburi has three major groups of *jao pho*.[34] The oldest group belongs to a wealthy retired lawyer. He entered politics in the late 1950s. He was returned as MP for Petchburi several times until 1979 when he left politics to develop his businesses. He became a senator in 1987 under the Prem government and remained in the senate until the end of the Chatichai government in 1991. His major business is now in real estate. One of his recent investments is a golf course in Cha-am. He wanted to run in the September 1992 election but in the end decided that he was too old.

The second group was headed by the late Somjit Puongmanee. He began his career as a truck driver. In his young days he was involved in a murder case, but with the help of another *jao pho* in Petchburi who had connections with a son of an army general, he managed to disentangle himself. Later he broke with the other *jao pho* who had helped him and the two became rivals. His gang was notorious for having a very brutal gunman and for having very powerful military connections. They were associated with Narong Kittikachorn, the third member of the Thanom-Praphat junta which ran the government in the 1960s, and with other high-ranking military officers.

The third group belongs to the A— family. P— A— has been an MP several times. His brother, Y—, has been an MP and a deputy minister of agriculture. Their cousin, P—k, was also an MP in the 1980s. They are known as *kok si kaki* or 'the khaki mob', a clear reference to their strong connections with the military and the police.

The three cousins are the fifth-generation descendants of a man who migrated from mainland China 'with one mat and one pillow' in the reign of King Rama IV. He married a local woman and one of his grandsons, Phum, became a lawyer working for the government during King Rama VI's reign. Phum was posted to Petchburi as a public prosecutor[35] and for his outstanding work he was given the honorific title of 'Khun' and a royally-bestowed surname. He later left government service, settled down in Petchburi, continued to practice law, and became a

major local figure. He had four wives and a large number of
children. Two of his sons, were active in politics and became MPs
for Petchburi in the 1940s and early 1950s.[36] One was also elected
mayor of Petchburi town.[37] It was alleged that he was notorious
for his love of gambling. He was close to Phao Sriyanon, the
director of police who was part of the group which seized power
by coup in 1947 and who came to be feared for his dictatorial use
of police power. It is alleged that in this period, the mayor's
followers ran a large-scale protection racket in Petchburi.[38]

The three current A— cousins started their political careers at
the local level. P— completed his early schooling in Petchburi
and went for secondary education in Bangkok at the leading
schools of the time, Amnuaysin and Suankulab. Among his
contemporaries at school were Dr Kamol Thongthammachat, Dr
Vijit Srisa-an and Narong Kittikachorn. On return to Petchburi, he
built up business interests including truck transportation,
passenger bus services, fishing boats and an ice factory.[39] P—
was elected a member of the municipality in 1967 and also
became president of the provincial council. In 1975 he was first
elected to the parliament and was subsequently returned again in
successive elections in 1979, 1983 and 1988. In the early 1980s he
helped the ex-premier, General Kriangsak Chomanan, to establish
the Chart Prachathipathai party. Later he switched his
allegiance to General Arthit and General Chavalit.[40] By the 1990s,
P— could boast of his ability to move around the notoriously
violent Petchburi province without bodyguards. 'I used to have
enemies', he claimed, 'but all of them have died.'[41]

Piya's younger brother, Y—, began his career as an accounts
clerk in a bank. After working there for 20 years and being
promoted a manager, he left to run businesses in salt panning
and shrimp farming. He had over 2,000 *rai* of land and set up a
trading company[42] His wife, B—, ran an ice factory and a bottled
water plant. Y— had an even more impressive career in local
politics than P—. He was elected member of the municipal
council (*samachik thesaban*) from 1967 to 1983, sat also on the
provincial council, and was elected mayor of Petchburi six times.
His faction was said to dominate elections at the local and
provincial level. After he moved into national politics, his wife

B— occupied the mayor's seat for another three terms.[43] In 1977 he was appointed a member of the national assembly (at this time the constitution was suspended following the 1976 coup), and was nominated to the senate in 1979. During the 1980s, he was secretary of the Ministry of Justice in one of the governments under Prem Tinsulanond.

A cousin, P—k was born in 1925. After completing his secondary education, he worked for the state railways and then went into rice trading. He entered local politics under the wing of his uncle. He was elected a member of the municipal council in 1967, and served as mayor from 1970 to 1974. P—k acquired a reputation of being a brave *nak leng* (*nak leng jai thung*) and had many followers. His wife is a capable and successful business women. One of his sons is a *phuyaiban* and leader of a youth group which helps to organize young voters at election times.[44]

The A— group is the most active group in local and national politics in Petchburi. They have had an edge over other candidates in local and national elections because of their wide connections, and an extensive network of informal influences established since the time of their forebears. Their success in national elections is as impressive as their record in local politics. P— was MP in 1975, 1979, 1983 and 1988; Y— in 1985, 1986 and 1992; P—k in 1983, 1986 and 1988. In 1983 and 1988 the three cousins swept the three-member slate for Petchburi. However, they were not invincible. P— failed to be elected in 1976 and again in 1986. P—k was defeated in March 1992. Through the 1980s, all three ran consistently as candidates of Chart Thai Party. In September 1992 P—k dropped out, P— remained with Chart Thai, but Y— ran under the banner of Chart Pattana, a breakaway from Chart Thai headed by General Chatichai. Despite running for different parties, P— and Y— still appeared on the same election posters.

In the September 1992 election, only Y— returned as an MP. P— lost to candidates of the Democrats (Alongkorn Polabutr) and Chart Pattana (Thani Yisan). One of the major reasons for P—'s loss was probably his overt support for the military action during the May incident in 1992 and his continued defence of the military action during his election campaign.[45] P—'s loss in the

September 1992 election says something about the vincibility of even the well-established *jao pho*. By early 1994, P— claimed that he had already begun campaigning for the next election: 'to date, I've spent hundreds of thousands of baht of my own money'.[46]

Narong Wongwan of Phrae. Narong Wongwan's grandfather was related to *jao muang Phrae*, the governor of the Phrae region under the traditional system in the nineteenth century. Through this connection the family subcontracted a lucrative teak concession from the East Asiatic Company. Narong's father also traded in rice and operated a saw mill. He later obtained a logging concession from the Thai government and extended the operation to other provinces including Payao, Chiang Rai (Amphoe Phang) and Chiang Mai (Maejam and Hangdong).

Narong was born in 1925 at around the time when the family business was doing well. Thus unlike other *jao pho* in our case studies, Narong received a good education. After completing secondary school in Thailand he went to the United States and obtained a degree in economics. Upon returning home he worked for the East Asiatic Company for a while and then entered the family business in saw milling. In the late 1950s he branched out into tobacco growing and curing. He expanded the curing businesses from Phrae to Chiang Rai, Chiang Mai and Lamphun.

Narong's rise from one of the most remote and backward areas of the country to the threshold of the premiership was founded on the tobacco plant. His family's status in Phrae and their connections in the local politics of the town made him a local figure of some importance. But the tobacco business broadened that into an electoral base which not only secured his own elections to parliament but also supported other candidates which formed the nucleus of his Ruam Thai party and the basis of his ability to bargain for ministerial office. In the 1970s, the tobacco business boomed throughout the northern provinces of Phrae, Chiang Mai, Chiang Rai and Lampang on the pull of growing export demand. Narong helped many of his relatives to establish curing plants throughout the tobacco tract. The curing plant owners provided the peasants with seeds, loans and other inputs, instructed them how to grow the tobacco, and bought the crop off them for hard cash. Strong demand and rising prices made this a profitable business for all involved, and a tight relationship developed between the curing plant owners and the growers. The plant owners became local wealthy élites who engaged in all kinds of public projects. These economic and personal relations between the curing plant owners and the people could easily be translated into votes for Narong and his associates at election time.[47]

The relatives on his father's side were active in politics and one was elected MP in 1969. Narong himself first entered local politics and was elected provincial council member of Phrae in 1949. From 1979 he was elected MP for Phrae continuously. By 1980 he obtained the post of deputy minister of interior. In 1981 he became deputy minister of agriculture, and rose to be minister in 1983. After the election in 1986 he was in the opposition. When Chatichai reshuffled his cabinet in 1990, Narong moved to the government side and was again appointed minister of agriculture.

In the early 1980s Narong headed his own small party, Ruam Thai, and bargained his support to gain entry to ministerships. Later he merged Ruam Thai with the Ekaparp (solidarity) party. After the military coup in 1991, Narong's name was included on the list of members of the preceding government who were accused of having become 'unusually rich' while in ministerial office. Shortly after, the coup group floated a new political party in preparation for the restoration of the constitution and new elections. Narong joined the group forming this Samakkhitham party, the charges of being 'unusually rich' were magically rescinded, and Narong went on to become the new party's leader. At the elections in March 1992, Samakkhitham won the highest number of seats in parliament, and Narong prepared to be elevated to the premiership at the head of a military-backed coalition of parties. At this point it was inconveniently revealed that Narong had once been denied a visa to enter the United States on grounds that he was suspected of involvement in narcotics. Narong had to step aside and allow the junta leader, General Suchinda, to be appointed premier.

The *jao pho* growth model

These five case studies show considerable variety. Extending the cases to include other provinces and other *jao pho* would only make the variety even greater. Even so, there are also commonalities. From the majority of the cases described above, it is possible to draw up a general account, a composite history, a model of the growth of a modern *jao pho* specific to Thailand in the 1980s and 1990s.

He is often ethnic Chinese, son of an immigrant family with a small trading business, and he receives only minimal education. He first starts to accumulate wealth in the upcountry businesses which boom from the 1960s onwards, particularly businesses associated with the rapid spread of cash crops. He soon moves into more profitable but risky areas such as mining and logging, and begins to build up contacts with the police, the military and other officials.

From here his career proceeds in two directions. On the one hand, he uses the cover of his powerful connections to move into illicit but highly profitable businesses such as illegal logging, smuggling, trade in arms and narcotics, gambling and extortion. To carry out these activities he becomes something of a gang leader with a following of gunmen and other associates. On the other hand, he starts to become a figure in local politics, which in turn opens up major opportunities in legal activities such as construction contracting and other businesses supported by public funds. With the backing of a local following, connections throughout local officialdom, and a base in local government, he is ideally placed to acquire a monopolistic position in many of the secondary businesses thrown up by the rising tide of urban growth. In particular he is well placed to become a major speculator in real estate, as well as extending into a range of service businesses (hotels, massage parlours, bus services, trucking) and distributorships (whisky, automobiles, petrol stations) supported by local demand. He manages some of these himself but also farms out others to his close lieutenants. By this point, he has acquired a local reputation as someone who can get things done, and he makes a point of sharing some of his considerable wealth both with those truly in need and with those whose influence or support may be of assistance to him.

Finally he is ready for the wider political stage. His contacts among local officials, businessmen and local politicians provide the network of *hua kanaen* (vote banks) necessary to deliver an electoral victory. Because of his own lack of education and perhaps also his own reluctance to enter the full glare of publicity, he will not stand for election himself but will lend his support to one or more local candidates. If his influence stretches over several constituencies, he is likely to be invited to take an official position within the organization of one of the political parties. But he may prefer to remain independent, to bargain his support with the national leaders, or simply to offer his services to the national leaders most likely to form the government.

With a network of contacts which now reaches from the parish pump to the cabinet office, he brings major new centrally-financed projects into the province. He gets the roads improved. He secures funding for wells, bridges, new electricity lines. He manages to bring in new local industry. All these successes add to his image as an influential man and a leader of the province.

Within this 'model', there are four major elements which will now be discussed further: first, the economic background of the *jao pho*'s spectacular business growth; second, the relationship between bureaucratic weakness and the growth of informal power; third, the opening up of local government; and finally the links between the *jao pho* and the structures of national politics.

The provincial boom. The development strategy adopted by the American-backed dictatorial government of General Sarit in the late 1950s provided the background for the explosive business success of the *jao pho*.[48] It stimulated growth based on the export of agricultural goods and the import of capital to establish new consumer goods industries. To promote agricultural expansion, it improved the communications network and irrigation in the old paddy-producing area of the central plain. It built an entirely new road network which opened up vast new areas of uplands cultivation in the northeast and the north.

Crop export boomed, both in the traditional crop of paddy and more especially in a range of new uplands crops including cassava, sugar, maize, tobacco and soya bean. This export boom opened up major new opportunities in crop trading, financing and processing. Many of the *jao pho* had interests in this area. One started out as a crop trader and developed major interests in rice and cassava. Another was a major force in the spread of tobacco in the north.

This boom prompted a rapid urban expansion in the provinces. Some old towns grew. But more particularly a number of new provincial centres rose rapidly from relative obscurity. This rapid urban growth opened up opportunities in construction, real estate, urban development, services and distribution. Moreover, because many of these boom towns were very new urban places with little or no developed urban élite, these new opportunities were open to anyone with the guts and ambition to seize them. It was possible for new men from humble backgrounds to ride this new urban escalator to wealth and influence.

This was very much a frontier style of economy with limited respect for law and convention, with high rewards for entrepreneurial flare, and with a very thin line drawn between legitimate business and various less legitimate practices. Construction contracting as a legal business is a common activity of the *jao pho*. Logging could be a perfectly legitimate concern but also had an illegal side which tended to offer higher returns. Real estate is a legal concern but could have an illegal side, involving access to use of land or possession of lands in forest reserves. Fishing also contained illegal and profitable opportunities. Mining as well. Meanwhile, the freewheeling new urban communities created other profitable illegal businesses particularly in smuggling, underground lotteries and other forms of gambling.

For many illegal business opportunities, location was critical and it is significant that many of the most notorious *jao pho* centres emerged either on the coasts or borders which offered opportunities for smuggling, or close to the forests which, with the right kind of protection, provided massive opportunities for illegal logging.

The combination of rapid growth in the provincial economy and the availability of highly profitable illegal business opportunities made it possible for entrepreneurs starting with very limited resources to achieve spectacular fortunes in a very short period. To take advantage of these opportunities, however, an entrepreneur needed to be sheltered from competitors and from the law.

The making of informal influence. To build up their informal influence in the local community, *jao pho* extend patronage to ordinary people including low-ranking officials; develop their own inner circle of friends, associates, dependants and assistants; and cultivate links with senior bureaucrats and military officers.

A typical *jao pho* extends his patronage generously among the ordinary villagers and low-ranking officials. A police officer famous for his moral stance recounted the difficulties he faced when sent to Chonburi to combat the influence (*itthiphon*) of the most notorious *jao pho* in the area:

'I was not given any manpower support... Originally the Police Director was going to give me about 20 extra men. But as soon as I arrived they [referring to an influential gang of *jao pho*] telephoned and sent telegrams to the minister, to the prime minister, to the MPs. Then the Police Director-General became afraid he may lose his post. He changed his mind and gave me only five extra men. This means I received half a person extra per district. With the exception of my personal secretary who sits outside my room, everyone else, behind me, on my side, including my superior are *their* [the *jao pho's*] men. Why? Because whenever these people have any problems they go to the *jao pho*. School opens, there is no money, they can get it from the *jao pho*... A pregnant wife about to deliver, has to go to the hospital, no money, go to see the *jao pho*, he gives the money needed... The extent of their patronage is incredible. People are indebted to their patronage [*bun khun*] up to their necks.'[49]

Kamnan Bo of Chonburi indeed boasted that he had more to offer than the local representatives of government:

'People cannot rely on *kharatchakan* [bureaucrats]. *Kharatchakan* have only small salaries. But I have much and I can distribute much. Whenever I sit in the local coffee shop [*ran kafae*] people can come and consult me. I am a man of the people already. I am more accessible than *kharatchakan*. On any matter where the *kharatchakan* cannot help, I can. And I do it willingly and quickly. It's all very convenient for people... Most of what I do is about giving employment and improving the local facilities.'[50]

The *jao pho* is careful to cultivate the image of himself as a *phu yai* or 'big man' concerned with the status and welfare of the community. He makes donations to local temples for building of new *ubosot* and *sala*. He regularly finances various types of religious trips and ceremonies (*thot pha pa, thot kathin*). He also gives donations to help government or semi-government infrastructure projects such as building roads, rest pavilions, bus shelters and bridges.

The *jao pho*'s informal influence is thus a function of the relative poverty of the mass of the people, the relatively poor state of local infrastructure, and the ineffectiveness of local systems for justice and social welfare. With moderate ease, the *jao pho* can provide some measure of security, justice, social welfare and local infrastructure more speedily and more accessibly than the official machinery. The *jao pho* stands out as a man of the locality, with great understanding and compassion for the local people.

Jao pho cannot survive without having a circle of close followers to look after their extensive business interests, both legal and illegal. Several *jao pho* have developed a system which can be called *thurakit upatham* (patronage business). The *jao pho* register their legal business enterprises under their own names, but will actually give their trusted associates a very free hand to run them on their behalf. The organization of the business is often loose and informal, allowing room for the managers to make money on the side. By this means *jao pho* can build up very widespread business empires as well as securing the loyalty of their associates, many of whom may also serve the *jao pho* as *nak leng* or gunmen. The business enterprises also provide jobs for other followers or those in need.

Besides followers, *jao pho* also need protection. The local authorities who possess the ability either to help or hinder their enterprises include police, military and civilian officials. For their obviously criminal activities in narcotics, smuggling, arms trade, gambling and illegal logging, the *jao pho* need protection or at least immunity from the highest levels of civilian and military authority in the locality. This might mean the commander of the regional army unit, the provincial governor, the district officer, and the chief of police. Official salaries remain low, making it moderately simple for an ambitious *jao pho* to offer even high officials very attractive inducements. Once they have squared the high authorities, they face few problems from their subordinates. One *jao pho* noted:

> 'Friends who studied with me years ago have now become "big" in various government agencies. I still keep in touch with them. They help me every time I have a problem. At present, several of them are in the Army, the Police Department and in the judicial branch.'[51]

The deployment of influence over local officials is well illustrated through the case of Nakhon Sawan, a thriving trading town at the northern edge of the central region. In the mid-1980s a leading *jao pho* with a base in forestry and logging allegedly eliminated all the leaders of rival gangs, and then took out insurance by bribing the police chiefs in each of the district's twelve *amphoe* (sub-districts) and won over the top police officer in the province by clandestinely running an underground lottery on the officer's behalf. According to the Ministry of Interior, this *jao pho* controlled the largest gambling den in town as well as other illegal activities. He then arranged the election success of a local politician, and after this politician had become a minister he used this connection to transfer a local official who was interfering with the *jao pho*'s land deals. This manoeuvre angered the provincial governor who came to the support of the transferred official. The *jao pho* promptly used his influence to attempt to remove the governor himself.[52]

The case studies above indicate the importance of connections with officials and with the military. One was helped by marrying into an official family. Another moved closely with military men and patronised military-linked politicians. The Petchaburi clan was locally known as 'the khaki mob' in reference to their extensive connections. One deputy police director summarised the nature of the typical *jao pho's* influence over officials in the following way:

> 'The structure of *jao pho's* power is like a pyramid. At the top is the *phu mi itthiphon* [men of influence]. At the left and right bases of the pyramid are hired gunmen and *kharatchakan* [government officials] who support the *jao pho*. If we pull the two bases of the pyramid away, namely the gunmen and the *kharatchakan*, the top of the pyramid will tumble because there is no other support.'[53]

Similarly Uthai Pimchaichon, MP for Chonburi, explained:

> 'At present the *phu mi itthiphon* [man of influence] in Chonburi, who is well known, will go around with only two types of people, the military or the police. This is to enhance his power to extort and intimidate the *chao ban* [villagers, ordinary people].'[54]

The *jao pho* and local politics. For the ambitious *jao pho*, opportunities in local government have three main attractions. First, they give access to several business opportunities, particularly in construction contracting, which may attract the *jao pho* personally or may simply be useful as patronage to bestow on others. Second, they contribute to the image of a *phu yai* or big man in the locality. Third, they provide a springboard for building connections with more important officials and for making the move up into the world of national politics. Many of the notorious *jao pho* who have financed candidates for parliament began their political careers at the local and provincial level, either with personal involvement or by supporting their favoured candidates.

Thailand's local government has a dual structure of officials and elected officials. Positions like the governor of the province, district officers and police are all appointed from the centre by the Ministry of Interior. These officials work alongside bodies of local representatives chosen by election in the locality. The provincial council or *sapha jangwat* is locally elected on a five-year term and has the power to approve the provincial budget and oversee the work of the governor and his staff. Each municipality is run by a mayor (*nayok thesamontri*) and municipal councillors, all elected on a four-year term. The municipality dispenses a relatively large budget amassed from local taxes and central subsidies, and control of the municipality conveys major patronage in the form of jobs and contracts. In the rural areas, the village headmen (*phuyaiban*) are elected by villagers, and the *kamnan* of a group of villages is in turn elected from among the *phuyaiban*, all on a lifetime basis. The *kamnan* in particular has considerable power as the executive arm of government at the local level in matters ranging from land registry to coordination of project work.

While this basic structure was initially established between the 1880s and the 1920s, its importance has increased significantly since the 1960s. With provincial urban growth, more municipalities have been created. With increased development expenditure, more funds have been channelled through the municipal and local budgets. In 1975 the government established a *tambon* development fund with the major task of improving local-level infrastructure. As president of the *tambon* council in charge of the disbursement of this fund, the *kamnan* has control over significant sums of government money.

The main concentrations of resources in this structure are in the municipal council budget under the control of the mayor and in the *tambon* fund under the *kamnan*. But the municipal councillors and the provincial councillors also are in a position to influence decisions. And besides the simple control over cash and patronage, local government office automatically conveys contacts with higher officialdom—with the governor, with visiting officials from the Ministry of Interior and other central bodies, and with the influential figures in the local military. Local businessmen understand that if they are elected to the local political positions such as *phuyaiban*, *kamnan*, provincial council member (*so jo*), mayor (*nayok thesamontri*) or municipal councillor, they will have access to new contacts and new business opportunities.

Because of the prospects of money to be made in local politics, there has been a high incidence of businessmen seeking the posts of provincial council members and *kamnan*. Of the 2,046 provincial councils elected in October 1990, 61.6 per cent reported their occupation as businessmen.[55] One of the more popular businesses of these candidates was construction contracting.[56] Similarly there is also a high incidence of mayors and municipal councillors engaging in real estate dealing, construction contracting and other businesses. Out of the 1,842 members elected to *thesaban* (municipal) councils in September 1990, 1,134 or 61.6 per cent reported their occupations as business and trading.[57]

Chartchai Na Chiangmai studied the network of influence in two rural areas of Chiang Mai in the late 1970s and early 1980s. He found that the *phuyaiban* of the two villages were rich before being elected to the post, and became richer and more powerful thereafter. They based their 'organizational reputation' on the control of gambling, illegally-produced whisky and slaughter-houses. In one of the villages the headman also was involved in the smuggling trade as part of the network of a powerful regional *jao pho* who had connections with government officials and teak buyers. Both headmen dominated the *tambon* fund development programme from budget to implementation. They had the complete control of the fund, so much so that they considered it their own personal domain.[58]

In a central region province close to Bangkok, the son of an ordinary trader was elected as a *phuyaiban* and *kamnan*, and worked so efficiently that he was named a model *kamnan*. When the government initiated a land development programme in the locality, involving earth moving, grading of the land and building of canals and roads, he set up a contracting company and carried out the projects from the government. By this means he quickly became wealthy. Subsequently his brother was elected as an MP and rose to the position of deputy minister. Through these political links the family began to engage in illegal logging from Burma and invested in the construction of a large hotel close to the Burmese border.

The *jao pho* and national politics. The *jao pho* have existed in provincial Thailand for many years, and were already growing rapidly in local influence from the 1960s onwards.[59] Yet at this period their influence was confined to their local arenas. From the mid-1970s onwards the *jao pho* very rapidly acquired a major role in national politics. Two changes accelerated this development: first, the military's extension of networks of support; and second, the extension of party politics under a system of parliamentary democracy.

From the mid-1930s to the mid-1970s, the military was the single most powerful institution in the Thai polity. After the events of 1973-76, many groups in the military became concerned that the power of the military institution was under attack and needed to be consolidated by building new bases of political support. In particular, the military groups were concerned that the assault on their power was coming from new groups in Bangkok—from students, workers, and even from businessmen who had previously been their allies. They set out to build new networks of support among important groups in the provincial areas.

In the mid to late 1970s, military groups helped found several new parapolitical organizations. One of the most successful was the Village Scouts which, as explained earlier, was designed as a grass roots organization through which people could show their support for the military against communism. Among those who were most attracted to this organization were some of the rising *jao pho*. Through such an organization, they could forge links with powerful military figures, and display these connections to personal effect. It was a favourite tactic to be photographed with a powerful general or similar figure, and to feature a large blow-up of the picture in a prominent place in the house. Moreover, through the various paramilitary groups formed by the military

in this period, the *jao pho* were able to acquire weapons for
arming their followers.

Such links between *jao pho* and military men became
significantly stronger in the 1980s in several ways. First, one
group in the military, headed by General Chavalit, set up the *Isan
Khiew* (Green Northeast) scheme designed to demonstrate
military leadership of rural development in rivalry with the
civilian government. Again the scheme provided an opportunity
for *jao pho* to demonstrate alignment with powerful military
figures. A northeastern *jao pho*, was one of its strongest
supporters. Second, several generals and other senior figures
entered parliament after their retirement. This appears to have
been part of a general policy designed to maintain some military
influence within the increasingly powerful parliament. Many of
these military men looked for electoral support to *jao pho* with
whom they had earlier been associated when they had been
provincial military commanders. Third, Sunthorn Kongsompong
who became commander-in-chief in 1988 and was the titular
leader of the coup in 1991, developed connections with many of
the nation's most prominent *jao pho*.

In the mid-1980s, the two military men who were most active
in forging links with the *jao pho* were General Sunthorn and
General Chavalit. After Prem vacated the premiership in 1988,
both these generals opposed the new prime minister, Chatichai,
but their strategies diverged. Chavalit retired from the army,
formed a political party (Kwamwangmai) and attempted to pull
in several of the major *jao pho* as his party organizers and
supporters in preparation for the next elections. Sunthorn
meanwhile opposed Chatichai using the military's more
traditional methods and led the junta which opposed Chatichai
by coup in February 1991. The coup junta (NPKC) then appears to
have attempted to break Chavalit's links with the *jao pho*. They
ordered the police to compile a list of *jao pho*, summoned several
of them for interviews at the Ministry of Interior, and in a few
cases (including an outraged Kamnan Bo) organized house
searches. They also closed down the *Isan Khiew* scheme which
had served as Chavalit's organizational link to the *jao pho*.

The linkages between the *jao pho* and the political parties represented a similar conjunction of mutual benefit. They were likewise initiated from the centre rather than from the provinces. Before the mid-1970s, electoral politics were of very limited importance. However, from the time of the establishment of a new constitution in 1975, parliament acquired significantly more power. Parliament operated briefly in 1975-76, was abrogated by coup, and reinstated by elections in 1979. Thereafter the parliament functioned without interruption for 12 years. Over this period, political parties developed to vie for power within the framework of parliamentary democracy.

By and large these parties originated in Bangkok among established political figures. But over 80 per cent of the parliamentary seats were returned from outside Bangkok. To be able to command enough support in parliament in order to have a role in government, a political party needed an electoral base in the provinces. The parties reached out into the provinces looking for electoral support and found the *jao pho* with appropriate networks of influence ready-made. For the most part the new parties did not establish national networks of party branch offices. They stayed in Bangkok and at each election went upcountry and tried to put together networks of *jao pho*.[60]

These links between politicians and the *jao pho* were generally forged on a personal basis. Kamnan Bo said he helped Boonchu Rojanasathian because he himself was a good friend of Boonchu's uncle and he felt it was his duty to promote such a dazzling local man. According to another source, Kamnan Bo helped Boonchu because someone he respected asked him in a way that he could not refuse for personal reasons. In the election of 1988, Bo put all his support behind candidates of Boonchu's Kitsangkom Party. On this he said: 'A *phu yai* (important and respected person) in the party has asked me to look after the candidates of Kitsangkom. And the candidates are also my relatives.'[61] He had also said elsewhere that the main reasons for his support were personal relations, and not anything to do with political party alignments. In his words: 'We go for friends and not for the party. This is the way of ours, countryfolks'.[62]

The *jao pho* used their networks of associates, contacts and dependents to serve as *hua kanaen* (vote banks) who could bring voters to the polling booths. On occasions, they might also use their influence over local officials to control the election result by more direct methods. Kamnan Bo admitted to having organized counterfeit voting. There have been many accusations of stuffed ballot boxes and other chicanery achieved through influence over the officials supervising the polls. Often, also, the *jao pho* would help fund the election campaign in the locality, and could even at times be persuaded to donate to the central party funds.

Just as with the contacts to military men, the *jao pho* welcomed this form of connection, partly as an indicator of their influence, partly as a new form of protection for their various activities, and partly for the new possibilities it opened up in business. Jongchai Tiengtham, a Chart Thai MP from Suphanburi, commented: 'Every *jao pho* has the backing of politicians.'[63] According to one *jao pho*, his interest in politics was motivated by his ambition to be famous. When he was a nobody he needed to raise his own social status, and make use of political links to further his business. He also had an ulterior motive in wanting to use his influence to help develop the locality, which would in turn enhance his own social and political relations within the community. In more recent years as he has achieved a certain social standing, he continued to sponsor electoral candidates to uphold his *saksi* or his dignified position.[64]

Higher social standing and prestige certainly have an economic pay-off. Opportunities to befriend politicians and to create a debt of gratitude help to build the *jao pho*'s ring of protection. As with donations to government projects and other charity organizations, *jao pho*'s connections with politicians reduce the likelihood that government officials will victimize them for their illegal activities. Further, *jao pho* who have their men elected into high places can manipulate the government machinery to extend their existing economic interests, both legal and illegal.[65]

The association between the political parties and the *jao pho* has also profoundly affected the parties themselves. While initially the provincial *jao pho* often agreed to support candidates preferred by the party leaders, subsequently they were able to use their power over the electoral process to impose their own choices on the parties. Kamnan Bo, for instance, initially gave his support to Boonchu, but later transferred it to a collection of local friends and relatives, and finally to his own sons. At the time when the political parties emerged in the 1970s, they largely represented personal interests and political attitudes which were relevant to Bangkok. Kitsangkom was an alliance between an enlightened conservative, Kukrit Pramoj, and some representatives of Bangkok big business such as Boonchu. The Chart Thai party was centred on the textile industry. The Democrats largely represented small and medium sized Bangkok business. Over the course of the 1980s, however, the major parties came to represent the interests of their key electoral base, the *jao pho*.

Initially the Chart Thai party was the most successful in building support amongst the *jao pho*. The party leaders were ex-military men who had gone into business, and perhaps they and the *jao pho* very easily reached mutual understanding on the possibilities of using politics to further business objectives. The Chart Thai party has found its major bases in the central region and in the northeast which have been major centres of *jao pho* influence. Overall the party has been the most successful in electoral terms since the early 1980s.[66] Kitsangkom shed its background amongst the enlightened conservatives and Bangkok business in the early 1980s, and emerged in mid-decade as a party of the *jao pho* of the central plain.

Regional patterns of *jao pho* influence

In 1991-2 the police drew up a list identifying *jao pho* in 39 out of the total of 76 provinces.[67] Out of the total of 256 names, 67 were found in the central region, 32 in the northeast, 11 in the north and 54 in the south.[68] These figures should not be taken as an accurate distribution. They do however indicate that *jao pho* can be found in every region. On closer examination, however, there are some clear regional differences not only in the incidence of *jao pho* but also in their style of operation and their impact on politics.

In the central region, the provinces of Samut Prakarn, Chonburi, Nonthaburi, Angthong, Pathumthani, Petchburi and Prachinburi have reputations as the seat of *jao pho*. Their main interests are gambling, contraband smuggling (including wood and arms), fishing, hotels, massage parlours and real estate. Some *jao pho* have their network of informal influence and businesses extending over several provinces. It is said that many of these *jao pho* are closely involved with the Chart Thai and Kitsangkom parties.[69] In this area, the level of violence perpetrated by the *jao pho* and their associates is relatively high. According to a police report, out of 735 known gunmen all over the country in 1991-2, over 300 are concentrated in Bangkok and the central region.

In the northeast region the most notorious *jao pho* have their bases in Khon Kaen, Ubon Ratchathani, Nakhon Phanom and Sakon Nakhon, and one widely powerful *jao pho* has a network of influence covering Roi-et, Loei, and Uttaradit. His major activities are gambling, logging, smuggling timber from neighbouring countries, buying and selling of cash crops, and real estate. In this region, the major *jao pho* tend not to lend their support to a single party but rather prefer to play the market. A leading *jao pho* was reported to support Kitprachakom at one time, then shifted to the Rassadorn Party led by Tienchai Sirisamphan, and in the September 1992 election worked for Kwamwangmai Party (New Aspiration) led by General Chavalit.

In the north, the major *jao pho* businesses are cash crops, logging, timber smuggling, and narcotics. Notorious local *jao pho* are reported in Lamphun, Lampang, Pitsanulok, Sukhothai, Uthaithani, Nakhon Sawan, Tak and Mae Hong Son. It is reported that some of these *jao pho* support Ekaparp and some smaller parties.

In the south, there is a group of old-time *jao pho* in the tin mining industry (known as *nai hua*) who are alleged to have extensive smuggling interests on the side. It was observed that before 1977, the 'modern' *jao pho* in this area were relatively inactive. This was probably the result of several causes. First, the area has a relatively long and developed urban history. The coastal centres in the south have been significant urban places for several centuries, in contrast to many of the upcountry towns in other regions which have risen over the last couple of generations. These southern towns have more established élites, which in turn has limited the possibilities open to new *jao pho* in the modern period. Second, the Communist Party of Thailand was exceptionally strong in the south in the late 1960s and early 1970s, and may have acted as a counterweight to the growth of new local potentates.[70] More recently there has been a growth of small-scale *jao pho* in the south involved in smuggling and other illegal businesses, particularly in Haad Yai, Phuket, Sungai Kolok and Nakhon Sithammarat.

The northern and southern regions have longer urban traditions and more well-established urban élites than the central area or the northeast. In the south, big and powerful families emerged in the nineteenth century with interests in tin mining and coastal trade. The state in this period confirmed their power by granting them tax-farming rights and drawing them into the bureaucracy. To a large extent they have survived as local élites to the present day. Similarly, in parts of the north, the old princely families, traditional noble families (*jao muang*) with major interests in land and other natural resources, and old tax-farming families have maintained local dominance into the present day. Moreover, both these areas have developed more of a civil society in the urban areas. This again appears to be a consequence of their relatively established urban traditions. People in the south in particular have shown more resistance to vote buying and other forms of influence which have allowed the *jao pho* to take a dominating role in electoral politics in other regions.

These areas still have petty *jao pho* whose business is totally criminal—particularly those involved in coastal and cross-border smuggling in the south, narcotics and cross-border smuggling in the north. But the existence of powerful established élites and something of an urban 'civil society' have restricted the ability of 'new men' to flourish on a blend of legitimate business, political influence and criminal activity.

By contrast, the towns of the northeast and the central plain are very new. In the central region, many came into existence in the late nineteenth century as trading centres and new administrative capitals. Until the 1960s, most had a population of only a few thousand. Their major expansion has come with the growth of upcountry commerce in the last three decades. Similarly in the northeast, a few regional centres have a long history but were still very small urban places until the 1960s, and have grown rapidly since then. These 'new' towns have been open areas of opportunity for new entrepreneurs who have been able to operate with little interference by established local élites and only limited supervision by the government.

Conclusion: *jao pho thai*, American bosses, Italian Mafia

The modern provincial *jao pho* are the creation of the extreme centralization of the Thai state on the one hand and the sudden growth of provincial wealth on the other. In the state system which was erected from the 1890s, power was concentrated in the ministries and barracks of Bangkok, while the provinces were controlled by a skeleton staff of governors and district officers aided by the occasional garrison and detachment of police. This worked well for some time because most of the wealth was in Bangkok. But once fortunes began to be made in the provinces at a spectacular rate from the 1950s onwards, the structure of provincial administration crumpled like paper. The relative lack of law and order allowed the 'new men' of provincial Thailand to make money exceptionally quickly through criminal activities and illicit methods. Moreover, once they had made their pile, they naturally set their sights on the capital where the real wealth, the real power and real action lay. They found it nearly impossible to penetrate the business life of the city, but much easier to penetrate its political world. Here the trigger was the political explosion of 1973-76 which destabilized the regime which had existed for the previous forty years, and sent both the old guard (the military) and the new guard (the political parties) scurrying off to the provinces in search of new allies and new bases of support.

Now *jao pho* are part of the political landscape. But how will they develop? Will they strengthen their grip on the political system? Or will they turn out to be a passing phase? In Italy the Mafia secured a stranglehold over the political system and retained it for more than a century. Only very recently has the extent of the Mafia's grip come fully to light. Only now are efforts being made to neutralize it, with no certainty of success. In the United States, the 'bosses' controlled politics for one generation. But then were pushed out. Is the situation of Thailand in the 1990s more like that in the United States or Italy?

Superficially there are many similarities between Thailand's emerging political system and that experienced by Italy in this century and especially since the Second World War. Recent revelations have shown how closely the Christian Democrat Party, which has dominated Italian politics since the war, has been involved with the Mafia and other local power centres. Several academic studies have shown how Italian elections work on a system of vote banks which is largely similar to the *hua kanaen* in Thailand.[71]

Yet there are optimistic reasons to believe that there are also some fundamental differences. In Italy the Mafia evolved in a situation in which power rested with the landlords and in which a centralized state and centralized authoritarian religious authority (the Catholic church) have tended to support landed wealth. Against the background of the Cold War, all attacks against landed wealth, central control and the Mafia's role have been too easily identified as 'communism'. In effect, the middle class has been recruited to support the system in which the Mafia flourishes for fear that any alternative will be far worse—the destruction of all private property, and levelling down at the hands of authoritarian communism. Meanwhile the extreme power of land, church and state created a stratum of the extreme poor who became the recruiting ground for the Mafia's armed power. The extreme gap between rich and poor created the environment in which corruption became an intrinsic part of political life.

Hopefully, Thailand lacks many of the basic features of the Italian paradigm. Thailand developed a centralized bureaucratic state with many similarities to the Italian state, but it has two key differences. First, the relationship between the Buddhist Sangha and the state in Thailand is very different from the role of Catholicism in Italy. Second, landlord power has been much less significant. Thailand has no historical alliance of state, large landlords, and religious establishment working together to oppress the peasantry. Until recently, Thailand was operating in a land-abundant, relatively resource-rich situation. The system of patron-clientelism and the cult of mafioso organization which emerged in oppressed, resource-scarce Italy has developed in a relatively mild form in Thailand.

In the United States[72] political patronage in the form of machine bossism developed from the mid-nineteenth century and continued to flourish into the 1920s and 1930s. Yet it dwindled in importance thereafter owing to changes in the economic positions of the beneficiaries (due to the opening up of economic opportunities and market forces), to the rise of countervailing forces critical of bossism, and to changes in the pattern of building political support bases at the local level.

Machine bossism was linked to the process of accelerated urbanization and to economic inequalities in the cities. It flourished in the periods of massive immigration into the United States from the mid-nineteenth century until the 1920s. The bosses organized votes among people who felt culturally distant from the dominant white Protestant élite, and who also felt discriminated against by them. The boss machines provided immigrants with unskilled jobs in the public sector, and awarded public contracts to contractors or businessmen who returned votes or material supports and gains to them. The bosses tried to make their dependents see the grant of a favour as generating a personal commitment that had to be maintained. But such commitment was only effective in the short or medium term, and eventually structural changes in the economic position of the beneficiaries undermined the possibility of building long-term links of dependence among them.

The great economic opportunities offered by the frontier economy in the United States quickly helped reduce the economic inequalities among the immigrant and other underprivileged groups, which was the basis of the success of bossism. The expansion of market forces, and increased roles for government in providing jobs in the mid-1930s spread economic prosperity, and led to a higher level of employment and rising wages in the private sector. The public programmes for social security, sickness and other forms of welfare further contributed to overall economic security. These socio-economic changes reduced the appeal of the patronage wielded by the bosses. Economic opportunity also helped immigrants integrate into the mainstream economic and social milieu.

Most important of all was the development of countervailing forces. Attacks were levelled against bossism from active sectors of 'public opinion' such as social reformers, civic associations, professionals and political circles. These people advocated the adoption of an institutional framework which would enhance equality, and encourage wider participation in the centres of power. In other words there was strong public pressure to make the political system more democratic. Criticism of bossism occurred even among people who had once been assisted by bosses and who had since been integrated into the mainstream of American society and adopted the American way of life. Eventually, the reformists were able to take control of the established political parties, especially the Democrat Party in the 1950s and 1960s. From this base they were able to engineer major changes in electoral practices and in local government. The decline of machine bossism, political patronage and other non-democratic political systems in the United States was ultimately brought about by the development of public opinion which viewed patronage and old systems of party loyalty as corrupt and politically inefficient. The countervailing forces arose among intellectual circles, reform and civic movements, and broader sectors of the population, both inside and outside political parties.

No doubt we would like to hope that the experiences of Thailand are more akin to those in the United States than in Italy. The economic history of Thailand is very different from the

United States, but Thailand also went through a process of 'frontier expansion' in the 1960s and 1970s. The relatively abundant land and natural resources have provided opportunities for people to advance themselves or change their status in the process of economic development. People could take the opportunities provided by the market.

This historical parallel to the American case of the 1930s may provide some measure of comfort but it provides no guarantee, and prescribes no time scale. Neither does it give any indication what may be the mechanisms for domesticating the *jao pho*.

But we may speculate about three. First, there may be an internal logic to the development cycle of the *jao pho* which will lead to an intrinsic change. In simple terms, once successful they may find good reasons to settle down and become respectable. The case study of Chonburi gives some indication of this process. In the 1960s and 1970s, the gangs of Kiang and Sia Jiew fought gun battles like petty outlaws. In the 1980s, their successor, Kamnan Bo, avoided any direct association with violence and developed a semi-respectable image. In the 1990s, his sons, who are now taking over the business and the political roles, are American educated. With a massive fortune behind them, they may have less inducement to take the risks with violence and corruption which built earlier *jao pho* careers. Indeed, their major objective may be to become pillars of society.

Second, there may be a growth of civil society in the provincial towns which denies the *jao pho* their political prominence. Here we can point to the example of the south, where the combination of more long-established élites and a more developed civil society have resulted in less prominence and less political influence of the *jao pho*. However, the process, is unlikely to be very quick.

Third, the big business community and the middle class of Bangkok is concerned about the growth of the *jao pho* and their corrupting impact on institutions of government and politics. While at present they appear to have little strategy for countering this influence, they at least possess the resources which could back such a strategy.[73]

At the elections of March and September 1992, certain groups based in the Bangkok middle class made a major effort to limit the impact of the *jao pho* on the electoral process. This effort arose because of a fear that the elections could result in a return of the coalition of military and *jao pho* interests which had led to the 1991-2 political crisis in the first place. Activist groups formed a PollWatch body which aimed to deny the *jao pho* their customary control over provincial elections. They campaigned for people to use their votes wisely and not to sell or otherwise alienate them to local political bosses. They stationed observers at polling stations in order to discourage obvious attempts at corruption, intimidation or tampering with the ballots.

The campaign had some measure of success. In the September 1992 election, several local politicians declined to stand. More sitting MPs were defeated than usual. Some notorious *jao pho* lost their seats. And Prachathipat (Democrat Party)—perhaps the least *jao pho* influenced of all the major parties—emerged as the leading party. However, the success should not be overestimated. The impact of PollWatch is hard to measure. The Democrat victory was exceptionally narrow. Had it not been for a factional quarrel between two cousins which split the Chart Thai party into two rival parties, the election result may have been very different.

While these factors may give us grounds for optimism, what can be done to accelerate the process of reducing the prevailing influence of *jao pho* on the political system? Three areas can be easily identified. First, as the American case indicates, anything which improves basic economic security and social justice for the mass of people will reduce the opportunities for *jao pho* to cultivate their informal influence as local *phu yai* (big men) who are more effective than government in solving local problems. This indicates the crucial importance of strategies which spread the benefits of economic growth more widely among the population, and of reforms in local administration which give people easier and fairer access to officialdom. This reform must be part of the democratic process which delegates power back to the people. Second, anything which improves the will and ability of the forces of law and order (the police, and the judiciary) to control the efforts of the *jao pho* to operate above the law will reduce the opportunities of the *jao pho* to build wealth on the basis of criminal activity and simultaneously to cultivate an image of invulnerability. This indicates the need for judicial reform, and for more social controls over the structure and performance of the police. Third, anything which helps to develop public opinion critical of *jao pho* power will ultimately reduce their freedom of operation. This indicates the need to cultivate the press, the NGOs and the pressure groups which oppose the exercise of *jao pho* power.

But it is also said that the biggest *jao pho* of all are those who hold top civilian and military positions and who lend support to the *jao pho* outside the government. What to do about them is the most difficult task of all.

Notes

1. Thanks are due to Thammakiat Kan-ari, Narong Petchprasert, Sombat Chantornvong, Somboon Suksamran and Ruth McVey for helpful comments and suggestions.

2. Bowring, Vol. 1 (1969: 86).

3. Luang Norakitborihan, *Anusorn nai ngan phraratchathan phloengsop sattrajan luang norakitborihan* [Cremation memorial volume of Luang Norakit Borihan], Rongphim Suanthongthin, Bangkok, 1977, cited in Tamada (1991).

4. Coughlin (1976: 136).

5. Sondhi (1991).

6. See a discussion of *nak leng* in the past in Anuman (1972: 381-400). The *nak leng* deteriorated quickly into local robbers with the inroads of commercialization, especially in the central region after the mid 19th century. See Suwit (1978: 182-186).

7. See Sombat (1992: 120-1).

8. It is in the nature of the subject that much of the evidence for these case studies is 'alleged'. The major sources are academic studies and newspaper reports supplemented by interviews. The alert reader should also look between the lines.

9. *Sia* is the Thai version of a Teochiu word for tycoon, and is often prefixed to the name of a Chinese-Thai who becomes wealthy from business.

10. 'Long Ju', a Taejew (Chaozhou) dialect word, means an executive manager.

11. Internal Security Operations Command evolved (1967) from the Communist Suppression Operations Command (CSOC), established by the Thai government in 1965. The agency was a combined civilian-police-military headquarters. It carried out a counterinsurgency campaign in the northeast, then the Communist Party of Thailand's stronghold. ISOC also engaged in anti-communist activities in other parts of the country. In recent years its budget and activities have been scaled down. It now operates under the National Security Council. See details in Saiyud Kerdphol, *The Struggle for Thailand: Counter-insurgency 1965-1985*, Bangkok: S. Research Center Co., Ltd. 1986.

12. *Matichon Sutsapda*, 4 March 1984.

13. 'Eliminating Dark Influences in Muang Chon', *Matichon Sutsapda*, 12 October 1986.

14. *Matichon Sutsapda*, 12 October 1986

15. *The Nation*, 7 April 1991.

16. *Matichon*, 7 January 1992.

17. This quote and a fuller account of the killing of Sia Huad appear in Anderson (1990: 47-48).

18. See *Thai Rath*, 23, 24 March 1993.

19. See Viengrat (1989).

20. *Matichon Sutsapda*, 25 May 1986.

21. *Matichon Sutsapda*, 25 May 1986.

22. This account is largely based on Ockey (1992: ch. 4).

23. See Somrudee (1991); Ockey (1993).

24. See '*Jao pho* in a Big Jam' in *The Nation*, 7 April 1991. When the Chat Taopoon casino was raided in May 1994, Sia Leng was present. The casino was alleged to be owned by him (*The Nation*, 21 May 1994).

25. *The Nation*, 7 April 1991, '*Jao pho*: Who's Who of Godfathers'.

26. *Naew Na*, 27 April 1990.

27. *Siam Rath*, 16 May 1990, quoted in '*Jak Sia Leng thung Kamnan Bo*' (From Sia Leng to Kamnan Bo), *Matichon Sutsapda*, 10 June 1990.

28. *Siam Rath*, 22 April 1990.

29. *Matichon Sutsapda*, 10 June 1990.

30. Banmuang, 17 April 1990, cited in '*Jak Sia Leng thung Kamnan Bo*' (From Sia Leng to Kamnan Bo), *Matichon Sutsapda*, 10 June 1990.

31. The MPs were: Kachornsak Srisawas (Roi-et), Vieng Vorachet (Roi-et), Unruen Areeeua (Roi-et), Suthat Sriratanapram (Khon Kaen), Arom

Pumpiriyapruen (Uttaradit). See *Naew Na*, May 1987; *Matichon Sutsapda*, 10 June 1990.

32. *Than Sethakit*, 21 January 1991.

33. *Krungthep Thurakit*, 14 July 1992.

34. Daily News, 19 May 1982.

35. Daily News, 21 July 1986.

36. *Than Sethakit*, 21 January 1991.

37. *Krungthep Thurakit*, 18 April 1992

38. *Krungthep Thurakit*, 14 July 1992.

39. *Krungthep Thurakit*, 21 July 1992.

40. *Dao Siam*, 6 February 1983.

41. *The Nation*, 19 May 1994.

42. *Than Sethakit*, 21 January 1991.

43. *Krungthep Thurakit*, 18 April 1992; *Matichon*, 6 October 1991.

44. *Matichon*, 6 October 1991.

45. *Krungthep Thurakit*, 26 August 1992.

46. *The Nation*, 19 May 1994.

47. See also the column *'Khunapap Sangkhom'* (The quality of society), *Thai Rath*, 31 March 1992.

48. See also Anderson (1990); Turton (1984).

49. Seri Temiyavej, in Pasuk and Sungsidh (1992: 147). Seri was *phu kamkabkan tamruat phuthorn* (provincial police superintendent) in Chonburi in 1986.

50. Viengrat (1989: 91).

51. *The Nation*, 19 May 1994.

52. *Matichon Sutsapda*, 25 March 1984.

53. *Thai Rath*, 12 May 1990.

54. *Naew Na*, 14 May 1990.

55. Somkiat (1993).

56. Ockey (1992: ch.3).

57. Somkiat (1993).

58. Chartchai (1983).

59. See also Sombat (1992); Suriyan (1990).

60. See Sombat (1992).

61. *Matichon*, 8 June 1988, cited in Sombat (1992: 132).

62. *Matichon Sutsapda*, 25 May 1986.

63. *Thai Rath*, 17 May 1990.

64. Viengrat (1989).

65. Sombat (1992: 128).

66. In 1992, Chatichai broke away from Chart Thai and formed a new party, Chart Pattana. He and his brother-in law, Pramarn Adireksarn, had tussled over the leadership of Chart Thai for some time. Besides, Chatichai was trying to capitalize on the electorate's wish, following the May 1992 crisis, for something new in politics, and was also trying to disassociate himself from Chart Thai's role in generating the crisis.

67. *Thai Rath*, 7 August 1991.

68. Preecha Sa-artsorn (1992).

69. And with the Samakkhitham party in the March 1992 election.

70. Thammakiat Kan-ari from *Matichon* Newspaper suggests this reasoning from his knowledge and experience of the south; interview, March 1993.

71. See for example Chubb (1982); 'Cleaning House' by Rod Nordland in *Newsweek*, 8 March 1993.

72. See Eisenstadt and Roniger (1984: especially 191-5).

73. As the first edition of this book went to press in mid-1994, three MPs become entangled in accusations of drug running, and one was arrested in an illegal casino.

4
CORRUPTION
IN
THE POLICE

The dignity, the discipline and the courage of the Thai police, we must protect. Even if we have to die in their defence.

Our flesh and our blood, we will sacrifice, for the happiness of the Thai people.

We are born to die. So we must leave good deeds for Thai people to remember us by.

We will help all Thais wherever they are. So wherever they are, Thais feel truly safe and happy.

The Police Song[1]

Images of the Thai Police

The police song paints an image which the police would like the society to share. The image which many people have of the police is very different. Many policemen are believed by the public to extort money, rape detainees, traffic in drugs, steal from public funds, acquire stolen property recovered by the state, and engage in all kinds of corruption willingly and without social conscience. In addition, many believe that senior police officers pay large sums of money to acquire the positions which enable them to indulge in these profitable activities. In an interview with the *Far Eastern Economic Review* in 1992, the prime minister Chuan Leekpai said:

> 'At the moment we are trying to get rid of officers who may have problems, in particular the transfers of police who in the past may have been involved in buying positions, going right up to the level of the minister. That is no longer the case. There is to a certain extent some deficiency in human resources in our police force. But the problem is also the system . . . that is why we propose to reform the system.'[2]

The prime minister accepted that purchasing of positions in the police hierarchy had happened 'in the past', but claimed that the practice was now defunct. A retired police general commented: 'I wonder where he obtained this information. And if he was in the opposition would he still be saying the same thing.'[3]

An academic who was once a police officer found that the income which the police received from extortion and protection had become fully institutionalized within the police force:

> 'The trickle-up benefits which government officials received from corruption syndicates *(tam nam)*... had a part to play... in creating cooperation within the police through the sharing of gains... In many cases such benefits were not used entirely for private benefits. They were also used as reserve funds which enabled high-ranking police officers to improve their work performance. The money was used to repair police stations, to buy office equipment, to decorate the office at times of festivities and important occasions, to pay for feasts on various occasions. The funds were used to pay for the cost of arranging welcoming parties for high-ranking police officers who visited the police station. They were also used to pay for miscellaneous items involved in investigative work and criminal cases, for purchasing tickets for charity events which the superiors or other organizations requested or forced the ordinary policemen to sell, as well as other emergency expenses.'[4]

To a large extent, the police appears still to operate along the principles of *gin muang*, the system of remuneration of officials which prevailed in the traditional bureaucracy. Krom Phraya Damrong Rachanuphap gave the following description of the *gin muang* system prior to the administrative reform in the 1880s:

> 'The principles of public administration known as *gin muang* are based on the idea that the governor (*jao muang*) must give up his private pursuits in order to administer matters of the state so that the people will live happily and without danger. Thus the people must repay this sacrifice with gratitude by helping him with his tasks or sharing with him goods which they produce or find, such as giving him the surplus of their own fish and other food. By this means the people relieve the governor of having to worry about his livelihood. With many people lending a helping hand, the governor can live comfortably. The central government does not have to pay his regular stipend. It is sufficient just to give him some fee in cash as expenses. His assistants (*krommakan*) will receive similar benefits, although less in accordance with their lower ranks... As for their livelihood, they are in a position to make use of their official posts to earn income better than anyone else... Thus there arose a widespread custom of earning an income from official positions.'[5]

This *gin muang* system is sometimes called *mao muang* or sub-contracting administration. The government subcontracted the tasks of tax collection and keeping of law and order to the governor and his men.

This system of subcontracting entailed low expenses on the part of the central government. In principle the governor could keep one third of the tax collected for his own use, and in practice the percentage might be more. In other cases the contract might specify a certain lump sum to be paid to the central government on an annual basis. What was obtained over and above the contractual amount, the governor and his men could keep as their own.

Krommakan were the assistants of the governor who carried out the actual work of tax collection. The governor recruited *krommakan* from well-to-do men in the locality, or from the local toughs (*nak leng*). The government did not have to pay these men regular stipends. Beyond their official duties, *krommakan* would exploit the people in the locality for their private gain. They made the people work on their rice land in return for protection from robbers. Some *krommakan* were leaders of robber gangs themselves. They shared in the loot from cattle and buffalo robbery. The governor and his men could then 'live comfortably'. The people were supposed to receive protection, but were likely to be exploited by paying excess taxes and also providing various unpaid goods and services.[6]

There are two major aspects of the *gin muang* system: first, the contractual arrangement between the central government and the governor to divide up the proceeds of tax collection; second, the systems which *krommakan* used to extract taxes from the people and pass them on to the governor. These principles continue to underlie the operations of the police force. It is alleged that police officers pay their superiors in order to advance up to more important positions. Subordinates are then held to extort money from the people on behalf of the officer. To ensure cooperation within the organization, the proceeds of venality are widely redistributed through the police hierarchy.

Such a system is similar to profit maximization, with men in the low ranks supplying the corruption money to the people higher up, going right up to the top, and in some periods in the past, to the minister. This became so well established that there is a popular saying:

'In the military, the superior gives money to the subordinates, but in the police, subordinates give money to the superior.'

According to one police officer: 'The system works as a redistribution mechanism. Money extorted from capitalists is redistributed to poor, low-ranking policemen.' In fact, those who provide the extortion money include many poor and underprivileged people, as well as modern-day slaves such as prostitutes. In addition, the major recipients of this money are top people in the police who may not be poor at all. Such a system defeats the main function of the police as a public office charged with the honourable job of providing law and order and maintaining justice in society.

Corruption permeates Thai administrative systems. By focusing on the police, we do not wish to imply that the police is a unique case, and that in other government departments such corruption is not important or absent. The police is chosen as a case study because in the opinion survey on the issue of public office and corruption (see chapter 5), the Police Department was perceived as the most corrupt among all government departments. The ultimate aim of this case study is to find ways to help the police improve their image and become worthy of the sentiments in the police song.

The historical roots of police corruption

The present state of alleged rampant corruption within the police must be understood in the context of the historical environment shaping the police's internal culture and operating practice.

The police existed since the Ayutthaya period. At that time their main duty was to provide security to the king. Sometimes they were used to patrol the outer fringes of the state. In the early Bangkok period, the police's main function was to marshal the king's men (*lek* and *phrai*) for doing corvée labour and military duty. When this *sakdina* system of labour control declined in the late nineteenth century, the police force also disappeared.

The development of the modern Thai police force began at the turn of the twentieth century. The story may be divided into two stages. The first stage runs from the establishment of the new police force in 1897 up to the Second World War. The second stage extends from the Cold War period to the present day.

The establishment of the police force was one element of the administrative reforms fashioned by King Chulalongkorn in the late nineteenth century. One of the main purposes of these reforms was to regularize and centralize the system of revenue collection, so as to reduce the leakage into the pockets of tax collectors under the *gin muang* system.

In the reforms, the king took away the function of taxation from local governors and their *krommakan*. He replaced these local officials with men appointed and controlled from Bangkok. These new bureaucrats were paid a regular salary and were no longer supposed to obtain their income from a percentage of the taxes they collected. The reforms met with strong resistance, both from the people who had to pay higher taxes in cash, and from the *krommakan* who used to benefit from the old system. Governors and *krommakan* often reacted by encouraging local toughs and robbers to create disturbances. Ordinary peasants revolted against the new taxation system. Thus immediately after the reforms, the government in Bangkok had to counter various types of local disturbances in faraway provinces.

According to a study by Viwanna, the government was not greatly concerned about the difficulties this lawlessness inflicted on the people. It was more concerned that local disturbances would provide a pretext for the British or the French to intervene in Thai affairs and annex territory in the name of restoring law and order. In 1888 and 1895 Thailand had to give up claims to sovereignty over territory on the east side of the Mekong River to France, and along the Salween River in the northwest to Britain. The colonial power used robbery and banditry as pretext to take over the territory on grounds of restoring law and order for the local people and for the smooth running of their businesses (particularly the British teak concessions in the north).

The fear that increases in local disturbances would lead to more such incidents led the government to set up a Police Department in 1897. The police was to be used first to control local influential men (governors and their gangs), second to act as an extension of the government arm in the provincial administration, and third to fend off colonial intrusion.

Viwanna concluded that the original purpose of the police force was first and foremost the maintenance of national security. From the beginning the police was created as an organization to suppress opposition to the government in power and to enhance the central government's interests. The police's function to safeguard the community was a secondary consideration.

Viwanna cited several incidents which showed that the police in this early period did not take its role as protector of people's safety very seriously. In 1897, Nakhon Chaisi was a major sugar producing area. Officials in this town had to turn a blind eye to the robbery of cattle and buffaloes because most of the sugar factory owners used these stolen beasts as work animals. If the police were to stop the robbery, sugar factories would have to be closed down, and the government revenue from the tax on sugar would cease.[7] In 1908 the government had to employ a large number of workers to build the railway to the north. The building had to be completed quickly for security reasons. Workers for the project had to be recruited from the northeast. They were an unruly lot. They drank, gambled, and robbed people. Local villagers living along the construction route were troubled by these toughs. The government was fully aware of the problems but did not take any action because labour was difficult to find. It feared that the workers would run away and the project would be delayed. Krom Phraya Damrong, who was then minister of interior, believed that after the construction was completed the problem would disappear of its own accord.[8]

The early police was also used to protect the government's business interests. In 1921 a dispute broke out between the government and the East Asiatic Company over the production of coal in Chumpon. Chao Phraya Yommarat, the director of police, ordered the police in the province to patrol the site of the dispute in order to protect the interests of the government which was the major shareholder of the coal mine. Chao Phraya Yommarat was overseeing the company on behalf of the government. The presence of the police was meant to intimidate the East Asiatic Company.[9]

Moreover, the conditions under which the early police force was created militated against the force functioning as protection for the community.

First, recruitment was difficult. In the beginning the government invested little funds in the police force. It recruited through conscription and paid low salaries. Living conditions were tough; many conscripts ran away. Later the government paid the police a regular salary, but the salary was still low and the problem of desertion persisted. Recruitment difficulties forced the government to accept people of low quality. According to Phraya Surasak, the police force in the early period was full of 'crooks, slaves evading work, opium addicts, alcoholics and junkies'.[10]

Second, virtually all of the police directors were appointed from the military. They ran the police like an army. In King Rama VI's time, the police director was chosen from men he could trust. The selection was not based on suitability in terms of previous training and other qualities.

Third, promotion criteria were irregular. Some policemen did not receive any promotion for many years. Some were totally unqualified but were promoted because of good connections.

Fourth, some policemen solved their low salary problems by becoming robbers themselves. Others abused their position and made money in various ways. For example, some police officers stole the salaries and allowances of their subordinates for their private use. Some extorted protection money from gambling house owners, opium dens and prostitutes. Fifth, the authorities were rather lenient in disciplining and punishing the police for fear that the police would not cooperate in the government's efforts to extend its authority over the upcountry provinces.

In sum, this early stage in the development of the police moulded a force which was designed to impose central authority rather than afford community protection; which was poorly paid and disciplined; and which still tended to live off the land in the style of *gin muang* administration.

The second stage in the development of the police force occurred in the context of the rise of military power after 1932, and more particularly from 1938 onwards. From the start, the main function of the police had been to protect the state and extend its power. After the military assumed control of the government, the security of the state became confused with the perpetuation of military-dominated government. The police came to be part of the mechanism to control or eliminate rivals or opponents of the political generals.

The police director and deputy directors continued to be appointed from the ranks of military officers. The new police

director after the coup in 1932 was Luang Adul Detjarat, one of
the leading army men who took part in the coup. After the coup
of 1947, General Phao Sriyanon, one of the leading members of
the coup group was appointed deputy director of police so that
'this would enable the government to arrest anyone who has no
faith in it'.[11] The minister of interior at the time objected to this
appointment but to no avail. Later General Phao was promoted
director of the police. While he held this post, 'many police tactics
were used [to eliminate political rivals]. The wives of offenders
were arrested to force the husband to relent. Mysterious deaths of
political prisoners under official arrest were common.'[12] In 1957,
Sarit again selected the police director, Prasert Ruchirawong,
from the ranks of the military. In addition, the police department
fell under the minister of interior who was regularly chosen from
among the leading political generals.

During the period of the Cold War (especially in the 1950s
and 1960s), the development of the police department was
influenced by anti-communist policies. The police was rejigged as
an organization to suppress communism. Foreign aid money was
poured into the police department in order to equip it with
modern technology to deal with insurgency. The police
department was boosted so much so that it was called the 'Fourth
Army'.[13] General Phao Sriyanon, the most notorious director of
the police at this time, created a squad of special aides known as
aswin waen phet (knights of the diamond ring), who basically
acted as his private hit men.

The increase in the power of the police also increased their
role as a predatory force. Corruption among the police was at its
height after 1947. Police in high positions were involved in all
levels of the drug trade.[14] Some senior police officers were
involved in the monopoly of the pig slaughtering business. They
used their position to make money from protection rackets of
various types, to siphon government funds into private
investment, and to receive nominal shares from companies. Some
also sold land and goods at exorbitant prices to the police
department. When General Praphat Charusathian was minister of
interior in overall charge of the police department, there were
many incidents involving corruption within the police

department. Some were revealed to the public as a result of the seizure of assets of Thanom-Praphat-Narong after they were asked to leave the country following the student uprising in 1973.[15]

Moreover, besides these examples of large-scale abuse of police power, the police continued to operate their *gin muang* style systems of extortion and protection. As Krom Phraya Damrong explained, the advantage of the *gin muang* system in the old days was that 'the government did not have to pay their stipend'. The government continued to pay the police low salaries and to provide inadequate funds for the maintenance of police stations and the provision of equipment. In effect, the government encouraged the police to develop supplementary pay and capital funding through private enterprise based on leveraging their official power.

According to a study by Purachai, many improvements made to police stations were not financed from the government budget. The police found the money themselves to pay for the costs. According to a study by Phongsan, police officers interpreted their low official salaries

'as a signal from the government that policemen must help themselves whatever way they could. Even honest policemen had to get supplementary income for their families. At the same time they witnessed the ways their superiors made money from their positions. Some of them might have expected some help from their superiors, but they were disappointed. They became frustrated.'

A police lieutenant general interviewed by Phongsan eventually 'decided to adapt himself to the system in order to cooperate for self-advancement'.[16]

In the Cold War period the government permitted the *gin muang* system to become very widespread, as part of the price for winning the police's cooperation for anti-communist operations. In this period, the systems for extorting money from the public and sharing them among police officers developed and formalized into elaborate networks of money flows. Sums collected from protection, from informal 'fines', from gifts, from payments for services rendered, were pooled and redistributed within sub-departments according to each individual officer's rank and connections. In this period also, the practice of buying the posts which commanded large shares from this trickle-up revenue also became more regularized.

The subculture of police corruption syndicates

By the time the communist threat faded in the 1980s, these networks had become firmly entrenched. A subculture within the police force had developed in order to perpetuate corruption. Acording to a thesis written by a police officer and based on a survey of police officers in the early 1980s, this subculture has several basic features. First, for a police officer to receive promotion and advance up the ladder quickly, he must please his boss in whatever way he can, whether legally or illegally.[17] Second, it is a custom and an obligation for a subordinate to provide a flow of money to his boss, and to provide help in other ways.[18] Third, advancement through favouritism, as part of the system of rewards for the favours which a subordinate provides to his boss, is considered normal and proper.[19] Fourth, 'gifts' of money to the police are considered acceptable as long as the people give 'willingly' and the police do not have to ask for them. These 'voluntary' donations are considered by the police as legitimate ways to supplement their low salaries and allowances.

The study by Phongsan describes the process which perpetuate this subculture. It begins at the police cadet school and is reinforced over the years through experience at work and through dealings with superiors who already possess the values of the subculture. Phongsan compares the young men beginning their study in the police cadet school to a 'white cloth'. They turn grey as they leave the school. After joining the police force, this grey colour grows darker over the years as they have to work with the superiors who live by the subculture, lack principles, and are intent on selfish gains. The rate at which the cloth darkens tends to accelerate with time.[20]

The results of the study on attitudes towards corruption reported in this volume (chapter 5) support Phongsan's findings. The researchers found that police officers came to accept the subculture as a result of being ordered to carry out the corrupt practices by their superiors. A high-ranking police officer noted that new recruits were rapidly absorbed into the subculture of corruption:

> 'If a new policeman is lucky, he may get a good boss. But most new policemen get to work under a bad boss, who will make him extort money, receive bribery, find money in whatever way he can. In this process a new policeman in the job quickly gets absorbed into the system.'

The subculture of corruption in the police force has been the target of criticism for many years. However, in the Cold War period, the government tended to evade this criticism for political reasons. As Cold War pressures eased in the mid-1970s, criticism became more intense. Elected MPs took up the issue. On 10 January 1980 the Administrative Committee (*khana kammathikan kan pokkhrong*) of the parliament clearly stated: 'At present the police department is hated and despised by all people outside it. This damage to the country is also caused by the inefficiency of the police.' In 1983 political parties of both the government and opposition pressed for the reform of the police. According to Pramarn Adireksarn, leader of the Chart Thai Party, 'the present structure and administration of the police department do not support the government policies and do not satisfy people's needs'.[21]

People who were victims of police corruption began reacting more violently to police misbehaviour. Some villagers set fire to a police station in protest against the death of a relative under police arrest. Owners of long-distance trucks joined together to obstruct a highway in protest against heavy police extortion.[22] The abbot of a provincial temple sent a petition complaining about police trying to extort money from him when he arranged a temple fair.[23]

From 1978 to 1986, reform of the police was under constant discussion by a series of governmental commissions. In 1981 and again in 1983, these bodies recommended plans for police reform. In 1981 these plans included shifting the police department from the supervision of the Ministry of Interior to the Office of the Prime Minister, allowing more supervision of the police at the provincial level, removing several administrative duties to other departments, and reducing the military character of the force. In 1983 the proposals included the establishment of national and provincial commissions to oversee the police, reducing the top-heaviness in the police hierarchy by cancelling several levels, and again removing administrative duties to other departments. On both occasions, the police entered strong objections to most of these measures. They feared that any alteration in the supervision of the police would bring in 'political' influences. They opposed any measures to rationalize the police hierarchy. They agreed only with the proposals to remove petty administrative duties to other departments. They insisted that the major problems of the police stemmed from inadequate training and manpower development.

On both occasions, the government showed little will to risk creating discontent in the police. The investigative commissions included heavy representations from the police and unsurprisingly failed to come up with radical proposals for restructuring the department. After the police had voiced their objections to the commission proposals, the governments backed away from any confrontation.[24]

Several studies have shown that the problem lies in the structure and operating practices of the police, rather than in the moral character of individual policemen.[25] Several initiatives to reform the police have run into strong opposition. There are many policemen who are not corrupt and who carry out their duties in an honest way. But the scale and breadth of the police subculture of alleged corruption ensures that large numbers of people have an interest in maintaining it, including politicians, bureaucrats from other ministries, and members of the judiciary.

Corruption at the police station[26]

The total police force numbers 170,000 in 1993. The director of
police is responsible to the Ministry of Interior. Under the
director, there are five deputy directors responsible for five lines
of work: for crime prevention and suppression; for special
activities; for administration; for internal security; and for
development. Each deputy director oversees work in his line of
command extending all over the kingdom. Apart from the five
deputy directors there are another eight assistants to the director
of the police.

The principal interface between the police and the public occurs at the police station. Each station has five sub-divisions responsible respectively for crime prevention and suppression
(mainly patrols); interrogation; investigation (mainly plain
clothes work); traffic control; clerical and administrative duties.
All the work at the police station is under the supervision of the
head police inspector (*sarawat yai*). Above the head police
inspector there is a complex hierarchy of command. Going up this
hierarchy, there is first a police superintendent who is usually
responsible for three police stations; next a police commander
who usually oversees more than 15 police stations; and then a
police commissioner, of whom there is one for each of the five
regions of the country (Bangkok Metropolis and central region,
east, northeast, north, south). Despite this complex network of
command, when things go wrong at the police station the head
police inspector is often the only person to bear the direct
responsibility. If inefficiency at the police station leads to criticism
of the police department, the police superintendent sometimes
will have to bear the responsibility and will be moved to other
areas. All the others on top of him are further removed in terms
of direct responsibility and are often not affected. For instance in
a notorious case in Songkhla in early 1993, a prostitute who ran
away from a brothel and hid in the town hall was murdered by a
policeman who worked in collusion with the brothel owner. The
head police inspector of the town was held responsible for the
police misdeed and was immediately moved out of Songkhla
province. No more senior officers were held to blame.

It is estimated that well over half of the regular policemen working in police stations are involved in syndicated corruption. Low-ranking policemen are alleged to collect money in various ways and pass it on to their seniors. The percentage of the policemen involved is held to be more at the bottom and less at the top. In other words not all of the top men are involved. But the number of those involved in syndicated corruption is large enough to overrule those who are not involved and who might want to suppress it. The main sources of revenue from corruption are considered to be:

Collection of protection money from gold shops, houses in remote suburbs, and factories.

Collection of fees from massage parlours, tea houses, bars, brothels and other places of illegal prostitution. Police have even been accused of abducting young girls from a brothel shortly before they were due to be rescued by a Crime Suppression Division squad. In one of these cases, it was only after a waiter in the brothel insisted that such an abduction had taken place that the police officer in charge radioed his subordinates to bring forward the girls.[27]

Collection of fees from illegal gambling dens and from legal operations such as snooker clubs which allow illegal gambling on the premises. Gambling dens exist even though the Ministry of Interior strictly prohibits them. The C— T— gambling den is a walled compound so large and so well-known that it is difficult to believe the police do not know of its existence. It was raided for the first time in May 1994. One MP figured among those netted, and several other MPs were rumoured to have left only shortly before the raid.[28]

Fees from the hired motorcycles which transport people into side lanes and along main roads. The riders pay a fee to a gang leader who in turn pays a regular sum to the police in the area. Without these pay-offs, they cannot operate freely as they are technically an illegal service. Similar fees are also extracted from local bus operators in upcountry towns.[29]

Pay-offs from illegal lotteries which are very widespread all over the country and earn the police a large sum on a monthly basis. Underground lotteries operate in cities, towns, villages, and temples. It is alleged that operators of underground lotteries must pay between 100,000-5,000,000 baht to the nearby local police unit every two weeks. For another kind of popular gambling game called *huey pingpong*, the payment per week is alleged to be in the order of 50,000-100,000 baht.[30]

Pay-offs for cooperating in the transportation of illegal logs and contraband of various kinds.

Charges on trucks which are loaded above the legal maximum. In an incident in early 1993, owners of big trucks (*sip lor*) in Prachuab Kirikhan and Chumpon provinces planned to close the highway connecting the two provinces in protest at the high rate of police extortion. An owner revealed that every truck passing the highway had to pay 250-300 baht to the highway police, and an additional 300-500 baht to the local police.[31]

Bribes paid by suspects in order to get away from the law. The amount held to be involved varies between 20,000 and 1,000,000 baht depending on the severity of the case.[32]

Extortion from drivers and motorcyclists for disobeying the traffic rules. Police officers often extract unofficial on-the-spot 'fines' from drivers who agree to pay rather than waste time and possibly incur a higher fine at the police station.

The police often describe these revenues as *kha sawatdikan* or 'welfare money'. A deputy police inspector described how he extracted payment:

'I try to raise some welfare money from factory owners in the locality. There are about 400-500 factories. I visit them to have a

chat, asking if they want the police to protect them. Late at night
they would fear some robbery. So I will make up a story that at
the moment a big robber gang is roaming around in the locality.
I ask for some welfare money in the form of petrol costs. Well, I
will make the man offer it himself. But the way we put it is that
we are giving them protection, helping them. So they contribute
willingly. . . Well, we have to create a scene to make it more
realistic, to make it work. We may use a catapult to smash their
windows, write a threatening letter, or intimidate them by
phone. Then we would send some policemen to guard their
place for a couple of nights. Then we tell them that we have
found the gang, who were our own men or they had run away.
Then they have trust in us. Well. . . we can actually protect them.
So they cough up the welfare money to help us do our work.'[33]

    This officer used the money he collected for private gain as
well as for furthering his work. He was promoted very quickly,
and he received four commendation awards for his outstanding
investigative work.
    The money-making power of a police post may extend
beyond the officer himself to his wife and other kin and
connections. Among the opportunities open to the wives of high-
ranking police officers are engaging in contraband trade,
collecting fees from subordinate officers in return for promotion
and other favours, and dealing in real estate.
    Position-buying operates at all levels of the police. A police
constable who wishes to be moved into a position which will
permit him to make money can realize his wish if he pays about
10,000 baht to the right person. For higher positions the money
involved varies from 50,000 baht for the lowest grade above the
constable to many million baht for higher positions such as
deputy police director and police director.
    Policemen may also pay to move sideways or upwards into
more lucrative geographical areas, such as areas with many bars,
massage parlours or gold shops.[34] Again, conservative estimates
suggest that these payments may run into six or seven figures for
a 'Grade A' zone. A police general of good repute said that in
1990 a good (i.e. lucrative) provincial police post could cost up to

one million baht.[35] In Bangkok in 1993, top positions were alleged to cost tens of millions. In 1994 the new police chief told the press he was investigating an alleged purchase of a high police position for 23 million baht.[36] Not all pay for promotion. A police officer with good connections may not need to pay to be promoted quickly to a desired post.

The many opportunities for corruption in matters relating to promotion and transfer result from very weak organization systems with no clear criteria and with wide powers allotted to the police director.

Conclusions and recommendations

From its inception, the Thai police has been an instrument of national security rather than a force for promoting the welfare and safety of the community. The government allowed the police to continue in the style of *gin muang* administration because it created a strong force at an economic cost. Being a policeman became a lucrative career. The police operated in many respects as a profit-maximizing enterprise. Extortion and protection rackets became the customary way for many policemen to supplement their incomes. Many bureaucrats and politicians shared in the loot the police extracted.

Because of national security considerations, the police have always been under the influence of the military. The police served the political interests of the military as a whole, and of particular military politicians as individuals. In return, the military governments allowed the police to continue their systems of informal revenue gathering. Under the military governments of the Cold War period, these systems became very extensive and regularized.

Corruption within the police force is held to be sustained by regular redistribution of revenues from corruption widely through the police force itself and through other related institutions. It is sustained also by a subculture which strengthens the group loyalty of those involved, legitimizes the acceptance of revenues from corruption as a form of supplementary income, and binds together vertical networks of bosses and subordinates who share the tasks of collecting and redistributing the revenue. The values of group loyalty and hierarchy which underlie this subculture are first nurtured in the police cadet school. They are further reinforced at work by the examples of other police officers and by the pressure from superiors and peers involved in the corruption networks. Not all policemen are involved in these networks. But the proportion which is corrupt is large enough to maintain the syndicate system.

The government has had little will to undermine this system. The government does not want to create discontent in the police force, and does not want to have to pay much more money to maintain it. Further, public pressure to contain police corruption has been weak and intermittent.

The practice of position-buying is facilitated by the systems of promotion and transfer. Indeed the systems of promotion and transfer may have evolved to facilitate position-buying. Senior postings are effectively decided by the police director alone. At lower levels of the hierarchy, superiors have similar absolute power, subject only to the counter-signature of those above them in the hierarchy. The system contains few checks and balances, and is inevitably suborned by the vertical corruption networks which characterize the police department.

The corruption syndicates within the police have been allowed to develop for four major reasons.

First, the revenue of these syndicates is widely distributed, not only among people in the police department, but also to other officials in the military, in the Ministry of Interior and in the juridical process of law enforcement.

Second, the system has been operative for a long period of time and had become embedded within a subculture which pervaded the police department. The police thus operates almost like 'a state within the state', which even the minister of interior and the prime minister find difficult to control.

Third, in the past the police had been used to serve private interests by higher bureaucrats and politicians in the name of 'national security'. The government itself neglected to provide adequate funds for its development. This forced the police to find their own means of support. Over time inadequate official funding became another reason for the proliferation of corruption practices.

Fourth, there has been no government with strong enough will to deal properly with the corruption syndicates within the police.

It is beyond our task to venture to offer prescriptions for controlling police corruption. Numerous committees, chaired even by deputy prime ministers, have been set up and charged with the task of finding ways to restructure and reform the police department. Useful recommendations have been made but never adopted. Generally they were rejected by the police department, often on ground of bad timing and unsuitability due to 'national security reasons'.[37] The proponents of reform have been unable to overcome the entrenched power of the police hierarchy.

In closing we would like to suggest three main issues for consideration relevant to the reform of the police.

First, there is a popular belief among bureaucrats both inside and outside the police that the police problem is easy to solve: if only we can recruit 'good' men with high moral principles then there will be no corrupt policemen. According to this view there is no need to restructure or reform the system of promotion and transfers; nor to decentralize the highly centralized structure of command within the police. This view emphasizes manpower development. This is an important aspect, but the reform of the 'structure' and the system is also crucial. Even prime minister Chuan Leekpai said that there is a need to restructure and reform the system. A good person working within a bad system can be easily suborned, because the temptation for lucrative gain is great. The power structure of the police must be decentralized, possibly along the lines adopted in Japan.

Second, the government through the prime minister must have a strong will to reform the police system. And the government must be able to guarantee safety to the people who make a stand against police wrong-doing. For instance, if the people are to stop paying bribes to the police, the government must come out to say so and help protect the people against reprisals from the police.

Third, a beginning could be made by setting up an independent body having the power to oversee the work of the police and impose serious punishment for wrongdoing. The model may be the clean-up of the corruption syndicates in the Hong Kong police in 1977.

Finally, it is important to stress again that the police is not different from other department of government. The historical pressures shaping the internal subculture of corruption in the police have had a similar impact on many other departments. Corruption in the police is especially noticeable because so many people come into contact with it in the course of their everyday lives. In our survey of popular opinion, the police department was rated as the most corrupt department of government. Corruption in the police also has a special significance. It encourages crime. It ensures that those who run illegal businesses and criminal activities can buy protection and make super-profits. This in turn leads to criminalization of both society and politics, since many of those who achieve wealth and power have risen from the super-profits of criminal activity. The appearance of suspected drug-runners and confessed big-time gamblers among the ranks of MPs is the result of police corruptibility, and has an impact on the image and the functioning of democratic institutions. One key pillar of democracy is the rule of the law and the opportunity of justice for all before the law. With a corrupt police, what we have is more like the rule of money and the opportunity of perverting justice for the benefit of the few.

Notes

1. In the 1960s this song was broadcast every morning on government radio stations. As a result, most Thai people in the age group of 40s upward can sing it by heart. It is still sung every morning by the police squad during their morning exercise around 6 am at one of the police units near Lumpini Park.

2. *Far Eastern Economic Review*, 5 August 1992, p. 20.

3. Interview with a retired police general on 16 August 1993.

4. Purachai (1983).

5. Damrong Rachanuphap (1952: 41-43).

6. See the discussion on *nak leng* in Anuman Rajadhon (1972), and Johnston (1980).

7. Phra Inthrathiban reported to King Chulalongkorn, cited in Viwanna (1984: 105).

8. Viwanna (1984: 103).

9. Viwanna (1984: 91).

10. Cited in Battye (1974: 302).

11. Cited in Sannathi (1989: 39).

12. Sannathi (1989: 41).

13. Sannathi (1989).

14. McCoy (1972).

15. For some details, see chapter 2.

16. Phongsan (1986: 217).

17. Phongsan (1986: 256).

18. Phongsan (1986: 275).

19. Phongsan (1986: 321).

20. Phongsan came to this conclusion after a series of in-depth interviews with 16 police officers. He collected information from their childhood right up through their schooling years and their careers at the police department. The sample ranged from police officers holding the lowest ranks up to the director of police.

21. Incidentally when Pramarn became minister of interior at a later date he did not succeed in reforming the police.

22. *Matichon*, daily, 10 March 1993.

23. *Matichon*, daily, 7 March 1993.

24. Sannathi (1989: 55-6, 71, 257-8).

25. In our focus group interviews among businessmen, we were told that some kind of syndicate corruption also exists in other government departments, such as the land department and the port authority.

26. The information in this section is supplied by an independent researcher, who does not wish to reveal his name. His everyday work requires him to work with the police at the police station. So the information obtained is from first-hand knowledge. The results of the findings were reported at a closed-door seminar, attended by two police generals, academics working on the police, and academic staff of the Faculty of Economics, Chulalongkorn University, on 10 August 1993. The participants at the closed-door seminar

were asked to comment on whether the findings were exaggerated or untrue. Following the comments and suggestions the report was revised and presented at an academic seminar at Chulalongkorn University on 24 July 1993.

27. See 'Local police abducted girl before CSD raid on brothel' in *The Nation*, 16 March 1994, pp. A1, A2.

28. *The Nation*, 21 May 1994.

29. Nucharin (1990) in a study of hired motor cycle services in Bangkok reports on kickbacks to the police. A group of residents of Amphoe Janhan in Roi-et requested the transfer of a police inspector because three police officers under him extorted 1,000-3,000 baht from small local bus operators *(rot song thaew)*. See *Matichon* daily, 10 March 1992, p. 21.

30. A study on underground lotteries found that an operator in an upcountry town paid 3,000 baht a month to the police station in the locality. An extra, uncertain sum was also paid to other police units in the area. Additional sums had to be paid to head police inspectors and other important police officers on special occasions such as end of the year celebration, Chinese new year, or when the police organized their special feasts. See Naruemon (1989).

31. *Matichon*, daily, 10 March 1993.

32. See Phongsan (1986: 295).

33. Phongsan (1986: 200).

34. The attractive areas classified by the police as 'Grade A' include Bangkok districts such as Bangrak, Phayathai, Pathumwan, Bang Sue, Lumpini, Bang Yi Rua, Phlapplachai, Jakkawat. Grade A places outside Bangkok include Nonthaburi, Pathumthani, Samut Prakarn, Chiang Mai, Khon Kaen, Ubon Ratchathani, Udon Thani, Nakhon Ratchasima, Nakhon Sithammarat, Songkhla.

35. Interview with a retired police general, 16 August 1993.

36. *Daily News*, 10 February 1994, p.1.

37. See Woradet (1983); Sannathi (1989).

5
PUBLIC ATTITUDES
TO CORRUPTION

What are the attitudes of Thai people towards corruption within the bureaucracy, and corruption among politicians? What factors have shaped these attitudes? What implications do they have for the political system?

These questions are here analysed using three sources of data: library research; a series of focus groups with different occupational groups; a questionnaire survey. The objective of the focus groups and questionnaire survey was to bring out *attitudes* towards corruption among different sections of the society. The survey was not a public poll or a referendum. The sample was not designed to be representative. The aim was to gain a broad, qualitative impression of attitudes.

The sampling for both the focus groups and the survey was constructed based on occupational groups, using the occupational classification in the National Statistical Office's Labour Force Surveys as a guide.[1] In addition, the samples were distributed by age, sex, and area. The survey covered Bangkok and the four regions, and within each region was distributed across large and small towns. The period of the research from the design of the questionnaires to the collection of information lasted from March 1992 to March 1993. In total 15,000 questionnaires were sent out and 2,243 were completed satisfactorily, giving a return rate of 15 per cent.

In addition to the survey, 35 focus groups (4-10 persons per group) were conducted among different occupational groups in

QUESTIONNAIRE SURVEY SAMPLE

The sampling was based on 19 occupational groups, which were then grouped into seven main categories. The sample of **businessmen** included owners, shareholders and senior executives of large companies, and also small and medium businessmen. The **middle class** sample included academics, media people, students, NGO workers, medical doctors, engineers, architects, managers and business professionals. The sample of **bureaucrats** included civil servants, military and police officers. **White collar** workers were drawn mainly from banking and financial companies. **Blue collar** workers came from industries such as textiles, metal and metal products, electrical and electronic. The sample of **urban poor** included vendors, slum dwellers, taxi drivers, barbers and general manual labourers. Finally the **farmers** category covered rice farmers, cash crop growers, vegetable and fruit gardeners, fishermen, village headmen and *tambon* headmen.

Occupation	Male	Female	Unknown	Total	Per cent
Businessmen	132	59	3	194	8.6
Politicians	32	4	3	39	1.7
Middle-class	285	279	2	566	25.2
Bureaucrats	300	183	4	487	21.7
White/blue collar	239	231	-	470	21.0
Urban poor	89	193	2	284	12.7
Farmers	122	79	2	203	9.1
Total	1199	1028	16	2243	100.0

Education	%	Region	%	Area	%	Age	%
Tertiary	46	Bangkok	35	Urban	83	<20	3
Secondary	19	Central	13	Rural	17	20-29	31
Vocational	17	North	14			30-39	34
Elementary	15	Northeast	14			40-49	21
No Education	1	East	4			50+	10
Others	2	West	2			Unknown	1
		South	15				
		Unknown	3				

different regions. The groups were conducted by trained moderators. For military and police officers, focus groups would not have worked because among such hierarchically organized occupations, even slight differences of rank can influence the expression of views. For these groups, we conducted face-to-face in-depth interviews with a sample of 47 people.

The bureaucracy and the concept of public office

The reform of the old administrative system into a modern bureaucracy begun by King Chulalongkorn in the 1880s led to changes in the functions of bureaucrats or *kharatchakan*. Under the old system of *sakdina* the old nobility or *khun nang* held the position of masters (*jao khon nai khon*) or big men (*phu yai*) giving protection and patronage to slaves and ordinary free men. The modern bureaucracy was theoretically built around the concept of public service provided by professional bureaucrats for the benefit of the citizenry.

Under the old system of the *sakdina* period, the *khun nang* did not receive a regular stipend. Instead, they were remunerated in several ways. They ran their own businesses, especially engaging in the junk trade with China and other countries. They gave protection and patronage to private enterprises (especially Chinese traders and tax-farmers) in return for an income. They extracted gifts and favours (*sin nam jai*) from the indentured peasants (*phrai*) under their control. They subtracted a percentage (conventionally one-tenth to one-third) from the taxes which they collected on behalf of the government. Within this system, *khun nang* operated as if they were the proprietors of the office, and as if the office was an asset which could be exploited for income. There was no separation between private and public domain. The *khun nang* derived their power from the king, and could legitimately use that power both to serve the king and to serve their own pecuniary interests. They worked for the state, and for themselves. The two domains were not at all separate.

While the *khun nang* were expected to take some 10-30 per cent of tax collections for their own use, many took much more.

One of the motivations for the reform of the administrative system by King Chulalongkorn was the desire to regularize revenue collection and to change the distribution between the government and the *khun nang*. In the reformed bureaucracy, *kharatchakan* were expected to work for the king, and the assets of the government were considered separate from their private domain. They became *khong luang*, the property of the king. But in fact the reforms did not erase the traditional power of the *khun nang*. They could still abuse their power and position. They still gave protection to merchants and traders. They still conducted their own privileged business enterprises, while at the same time functioning as government officials.

The revolution in 1932 abolished the absolute monarchy and shifted power from the monarchy to a group of military and bureaucrats. Between 1932 and 1973 the public administration was truly in the hands of the bureaucracy, hence the rise of the description 'bureaucratic polity'. In this period some emphasis was given to the idea that bureaucrats must work for the benefit of the people, and that government administration was a 'public office'. Yet this concept was far from firmly entrenched. The re-assertion of the power of the monarchy, made possible with the rise of Sarit Thanarat in 1957, revitalized the ideology of absolutist rule according to which all governmental authority descended from the absolute power of the king, which in turn was based on the king's uniquely infinite store of accumulated merit (*bun*). Sarit fashioned the role of the military as the protector of 'nation, religion and king'. The military claimed the moral right and legitimacy to rule on behalf of the king. This ideology sustained the idea that the public administration functioned for the benefit of the king.

The concept of 'public office' has been weak in Thai society. The public have not absorbed the concept of 'public office' and hence have failed to protect their rights. This weakness has permitted government officials to exploit power and position for private gain. Officials have succeeded in sustaining traditional conceptions of their own role, and traditional conceptions of the proper deference they deserve. Ordinary people still look up to government officials as patrons or masters. They are not properly aware of their rights to receive public service under the concept of modern administration. They continue to regard these services as favours which the powerful deign to bestow on their inferiors, the powerless ordinary people.

Attitudes towards corruption and public office

In Thai there are several different phrases to describe a non-official payment to an official. In focus groups, we probed the meaning of these different phrases and asked respondents to arrange them in rank order. From least to most severe, the order was as follows:

least severe	*sin nam jai*	gift of good will
	kha nam ron nam cha	tea money
	praphuet mi chob	improper behaviour
	sin bon, rit thai	bribery, extortion
	thut jarit to nathi	dishonesty in duty
most severe	*kan khorrapchan*	corruption

At one end of the spectrum, the phrase *sin nam jai* implies a traditional form of showing gratitude, typically applicable within the context of a patron-client style of relationship. At the other end, the word *khorrapchan* has been inducted into Thai from English to describe payments which are without doubt morally wrong, and possibly also criminal and socially destructive.

To examine attitudes towards the concept of public office, we asked sample respondents about their reaction to several hypothetical situations involving the payment of money to officials. In each case, the respondents were invited to choose from a pre-set list of possible answers; and they could select one or several. To understand the logic which lay behind the answers, we raised the same hypothetical situations during the qualitative group discussions, and probed at length.

In this chapter, we present only summaries of the questionnaire results. Fuller tabulations can be found in the Thai version of this book.[2] For all questions, multiple answers were allowed; the percentages are based on the full final sample of 2,243 respondents.

To avoid having to visit the police station and pay a full fine, a traffic offender offers to pay a 'fine' directly to a traffic policeman. The policeman did not ask for the money, but accepted it. How do you regard this incident?

		Per cent
a)	Bribery *(sin bon)*	61.0
b)	Improper behaviour *(praphuet mi chob)*	36.6
c)	Dishonesty in duty *(thut jarit to nathi)*	31.4
d)	Corruption *(khorrapchan)*	15.6
e)	Not corruption	5.1
f)	No answers, others	8.9

Very few consider it 'corruption' to allow a police officer to appropriate the fine paid for a minor traffic offence. This is because the sum of money involved is small, the offender initiates the transaction, and the policeman does not actively solicit the money. The offender is buying convenience. A businessman from Chonburi commented: 'This is only a small thing, I do not think it will stop the traffic or anything'. A university student said, '*sin bon* [bribery] is not a serious offence. It is not like corruption which is a serious offence'. According to a soldier, this transaction is not corruption because 'the policeman does not ask for it, and the briber uses his own money not public money'. A civil servant argued that it is not corruption because the sum involved is small and the policeman does not ask for it. However, if the sum had been larger and the policeman had asked for it, then it would qualify as corruption. This respondent summed up:

> 'We want convenience. We know it is wrong. But if we have to go to the police station, we do not know where it is. [At the station] we would pay 4-600 baht. If we give the policeman 100 or 50 baht, we do not feel it is corruption. Also the policeman did not insist we have to give him the money. It may be a kind of corruption, but not a serious one because it does not cause

any damage. But if the policeman asked for a lot of money, it would be considered corruption.'

The higher the education of the respondents the greater the tendency to view police action as *sin bon* or bribery. Those 15.6 per cent of total respondents who do consider this action as 'corruption' base their judgement on a strict approach to the law. They believe that the action is 'corruption' because the policeman 'does not adhere to the law', or 'is negligent of his duties according to the law'.

Among the sub-sample of government officials, the proportion who judge this action as 'corruption' is only 10 per cent, below the average for the total sample. Among the sub-sample of policemen, it is even lower at 5 per cent. Some 45 percent of policemen called it 'bribery', 34 per cent 'improper behaviour', and 27 per cent 'dishonesty'. Policemen appear to recognize that the action is wrong but not serious. They rationalize that the giver 'willingly' offers the money.

A person visits a government office, and receives good assistance from the officer in charge. When the matter is concluded, he offers 50 baht which the government official accepts. How would you describe this behaviour?

		Per cent
a)	Gift of good will (*sin nam jai*)	70.1
b)	Tea money (*kha nam ron nam cha*)	16.8
c)	Dishonesty in duty (*thut jarit to nathi*)	8.1
d)	Bribery (*sin bon*)	18.6
d)	Corruption (*khorrapchan*)	4.5
e)	No answers, others	7.9

Respondents overwhelmingly felt that a small payment to a government official as recognition for services performed was a 'gift of good will' with no pejorative connotations. Only 16.8 per cent applied the gently critical term of 'tea money', only 8.1 per cent considered it a dishonest dereliction of duty, and only 4.5

percent felt it merited the term 'corruption'. The distribution of answers was relatively constant across different sub-samples.

Businessmen reasoned that giving money to a government official is a gift of good will because this shows one's gratitude for the assistance the official provided: 'Ten or 20 baht is a show of thanks. Okay, he helps us, there is no problem about that, but he must not bend the rules.' Another businessman said: 'As long as we don't offer the money in order to get some benefit or to influence the official, then it is purely a sign of thanks, a *sin nam jai*, it is not corruption.' Another small businessman reasoned that he had to deal with government offices all the time, so he knew a lot of officials, and received very good service from them. In return he felt bound to offer them some compensation, partly because he knew officials receive low salaries.

Slum dwellers and farmers noted that sometimes they could not fill out forms or understand official documents themselves, and they would pay *sin nam jai* as thanks to the officials who helped them. These payments were by way of 'thanking him for facilitating the affair'.

Civil servants and police officers regard the behaviour as *sin nam jai* because the giver is willing, and the receiver 'receives this willingness' or 'receives this tip' from the people without condition. They contend that this behaviour entails no undue harm to society.

Middle-class professionals including academics, media personnel, NGO workers, and other take a tougher view of this kind of action. A quarter of them label the payment as 'tea money', and 10.1 per cent call it a dishonest dereliction of duty. Still only a small number, 6.4 per cent, state it is corruption. These critics consider it the 'duty' of the government officials to carry on their work, the public should not offer the money, and the officials should not accept it. One academic stated: 'It is his job to give the service. There is no need for us to pay him extra.' Another said: 'A good government official should not receive the money. He can refuse the offer. He should not accept the money for just doing his duty.'

The few who apply the term corruption come especially from the ranks of NGO workers, academics, and media professionals. They argue that the gift perverts the relationship between officialdom and the public: 'It is wrong. It should not be done. Receiving money is totally wrong.' The offer of money subverts the official. The acceptance of the money indicates that the official does not understand the concept of official duty. The practice creates a habit among officials. Government officials get used to the practice and in the end will not perform their duties unless they receive tea money.

If an official deliberately works slowly in order to pressure people into paying money for faster service, a little under half of respondents use lightly critical terms such as 'dishonesty in work' or 'tea money'. They feel that this behaviour is tolerable or only slightly wrong because the person is 'buying convenience', and because 'the government official does not ask for it, we give the money ourselves'. Some rationalise that 'it is a mutual thing', implicitly accepting that the official has the ability if not the right to make some small private profit from his official position.

A person needs some service from a government department. The officer in charge deliberately takes his time. The person gives the officer money (20-100 baht) to speed up the work and to reward the officer for his efforts (*kha noey*). How do you describe this behaviour?

	Per cent
a) A gift of good will (*sin nam jai*)	5.6
b) Dishonest in duty (*thut jarit to nathi*)	23.6
c) Tea money (*kha nam ron nam cha*)	19.9
d) Bribery (*sin bon*)	56.4
e) Extortion (*rit thai*)	18.5
e) Corruption (*khorrapchan*)	15.8
f) No answer, others	5.9

Businessmen see the practice as 'buying convenience' and 'part of the cost of running a business'. They accept the need to pay for 'the assistance given by government officials' in order to 'quicken the procedure, facilitate the matter'. A seller of building materials from Songkhla said: 'It is just our generosity to give him some money; we cannot blame the official.' A real estate dealer from Nakhon Sithammarat also said: 'I do not think this is corruption, because the official did not ask for it. We give it to him willingly so that things will be more convenient for us, so that we can have extra time to do other things. We do not ask him to do anything against the rules. We ask him to do the things he needs to do anyway. Its nothing wrong, it's just faster.'

Many government officials argue that there is little or nothing wrong in a payment intended to buy some extra speed. Government officials may have so much work that they have to work outside hours, for which they receive no overtime.

For many, however, this behaviour by the official indicates a dishonest *intention*, and hence they are more critical. Only a very small number considered such forced payments as *sin nam jai*. Over half used the term bribery. In all 15.8 per cent used the term corruption.

Professional people tend to call this behaviour as *sin bon* (bribery) or *rit thai* (extortion) which implies that it is wrong but not so bad as to merit the term corruption. Like the businessmen, they recognize that 'it is the cost of quickening the process without asking the official to bend the rules or to turn wrong into right'. The practice causes no harm to government, but does entail some social cost: 'It is jumping the queue. The person who does it is exploiting others in society.'

Administrative corruption

The Thai term *bang luang* refers to the ways civil bureaucrats make use of government office to acquire private gains through moonlighting, receiving commission fees or kickbacks, abusing government property, and using their powerful position to help friends and relatives.

Almost half of the sample stated that an official pilfering even small articles such as pencils and paper from a government office amounts to corruption. However, slightly over half called it merely 'improper behaviour', implying that it is technically incorrect but nevertheless tolerable since the small values involved cause little social hurt: 'According to the rules and regulations it is corruption. But generally in the case of such small things, we find it tolerable'.

If a government official takes paper and pencils from the office to use at home, what do you call it?	Per cent
a) Improper behaviour	52.5
b) Dishonesty in his work	15.8
c) Corruption	48.6
d) Not corruption	4.9
e) No answer, others	8.5

More of the slum dwellers, farmers and blue collar workers call the behaviour 'improper' as compared to the businessmen and officials. These lower-echelon respondents argued that though the individual offence was small, the potential damage was large. If every government official did it every day, then the accumulated leakage would amount to billions of baht. Moreover, government property is purchased with the tax money of the people. Thus government officials should not treat it as if it were their private property.

The middle class groups condemn such official pilfering most heavily. Almost three-fifths described the practice as corruption. They contend that government property belongs to the public, no matter how small the value may be. If government officials treat it as a private possession, then this amounts to stealing from the public and demeans the moral standing of officialdom.

Politicians are most lenient to government officials on this score. Almost a quarter of the politicians surveyed argued that such pilfering could definitely not be labelled corruption, on grounds that the values involved are small. One MP said: 'Taking a public thing for personal use is dishonest. But I live in the real world. Even if this is wrong, it is only a little wrong.'

142

CORRUPTION AND DEMOCRACY IN THAILAND

Another MP said: 'I think what you talk about is only a small wound. But most of what goes on in the government are enormous wounds. So we do not see the small wound as corruption. If there is no wound at all we will see even a small wound as corruption. But as it is we do not see it.'

Next we asked a similar question about a government official using an official car for private purposes. Compared to the pencil-and-paper example, the proportion rating this as corruption rises from 48.6 to 59.0 per cent. The increase is sharpest among the lower-echelon groups of urban poor, farmers and blue collar workers. Among this group, the larger value of the property involved sharpens their critical perceptions. A fisherman from Chonburi said: 'This is corruption, or cheating from the public coffers.' A farmer from Lopburi said: 'These things are government property. The official intended to cheat. Petrol can be sold for money.' Among businessmen and middle-class groups, the proportion also rises slightly. Among government officials, there is least change.

A government official uses an official car and petrol for personal affairs. How do you describe this behaviour?

	Per cent
a) Improper behaviour	48.0
b) Dishonesty in duty	22.1
c) Corruption	59.0
d) Not corruption	1.8
e) No answer, others	6.4

Officials and private business. Under the modern concept of bureaucracy in the west, government officials are public persons who provide public services. By implication, government officials should not have positions in private companies, because they may be able to use the power entrusted to them by the public for the private advantage of themselves and the companies to which they are connected. Thus officials who depart from this principle may be considered corrupt.

Since the rise of military power in the late 1930s, companies have customarily invited high-ranking and influential military and police officers to sit on their boards of directors or advisory boards. The practice increased sharply after the coup in 1947. It diminished after the fall of the military government in 1973 but far from completely. After the coup by the NPKC in 1991, many military officers associated with the NPKC were invited to sit on corporate boards, especially those of golf courses, resorts and real estate companies which needed influence to negotiate the land laws. Critics have argued that these connections pervert the market and allow companies to flaunt laws and regulations. In a press interview, General Suchinda Kraprayun, a leading member of the NPKC, said that such behaviour by military officers was acceptable because there was no law which prohibits government officials from being board members or advisors of private companies.

If senior military/police officers become advisors or board members of private companies while still in office, how do you describe this behaviour?

	Per cent
a) Normal state of affairs/lawful	28.0
b) Inappropriate behaviour	61.4
c) Corruption	4.6
d) No answer, others	14.9

Among the respondents, just over three-fifths felt it was 'inappropriate behaviour' (*phruettikan thi mai khuan kratham*) for government officials to sit on the boards of private companies. Only 5 per cent thought it was corruption, and a quarter argued that it was perfectly legal and normal.

The proportion classifying this behaviour as improper is highest (72.2 per cent) amongst businessmen. On probing, it emerges that they resent 'influential companies' which receive protection to do illegal things such as encroaching on national forest reserves, or making use of the office hours of high-ranking government officials at public expense. A construction contractor said:

'If we let high-ranking government officials sit as presidents of boards of private firms, this will create problems with regards to rules and regulations. The official gives protection to the company so it can bend the rules. This type of thing causes a lot of damage to the country. For instance a company building a golf course will buy hundreds of *rai* of land, encroaching on the national forest reserves. But no one dares to touch the company. This practice destroys the system of public administration.'

But businessmen do not call this practice corruption. They consider it 'not right', 'improper', 'should not be done', and 'a protection racket'. Meanwhile politicians recognize that even though the practice is not against the law, it is wrong on grounds of legitimacy and morality. A good military officer should not use public time to help private firms. An MP from Nakhon Sithammarat said: 'Even if it is not a clear case of corruption, I would say the time a military man spent on business affairs amounts to cheating with public time... High-ranking government officers can use their powerful positions to benefit these private companies.'

The attitude of the middle class groups is broadly similar. According to one academic respondent:

'Just by lending his name, the company can already gain some benefit. In reality if you are the owner of a golf course, your name will not be influential enough to prevent villagers from protesting against you. But if the head of the army is the president of the board of directors of this golf course, who would dare to protest? Even to criticize this golf course company, no one dares. The officer who accepts such an appointment knows full well its implications. If Suchinda is not the head of the army who would want him to be the president of a golf course company?'

People in the lower social echelons are more tolerant of or resigned to this practice. They consider it normal. First, they have become inured to the fact that powerful people exploit their positions in this way. A worker from a state enterprise said: 'I consider it a personal right. It is acceptable if he does not use the government working hours. But in the future we must see if he engages in corruption. We cannot associate influential people with corruption automatically. Sometimes they do not do any-thing, but people are already scared.' Second, they reason that government officials should be able to work outside office hours on private matters.

Third, they argue that the private company's invitation to the officer to sit on the board is evidence that the officer is a good man, reputable or influential. A farmer from Lopburi said: 'He is good and that is why the company appoints him. One cannot say the company hires him.' A village headman from Chiang Mai said: 'Private companies appoint high officials for good image. I do not consider it corruption.'

Fourth, they accept that it is a customary practice for private companies to seek patrons among influential government officials. A worker from a state enterprise in Songkhla said: 'I do not think it corruption because in Thai society we must have protection from big bosses [*luk phi*]. If this government official is a good man but has his name on the board of a company, anyone seeing this name feels respectful towards this company. Further this practice makes the company more secure from the beginning.'

Among government officials, the military are the most likely to consider this practice normal. Civilian officials and policemen are less sure. Military men believe the relationship between military officers, influential political people and business is part of 'giving each other honour, helping one another'. They argue that 'it is a private matter', and 'businessmen need a patron'. An army colonel said:

'Sometimes people have done favours for one another, and they have become close. This person used to help us, we like him. He wants to use our name as president of his board. Sometimes we have to consent. Because in our society we are not so individualistic like westerners. Thai people live together like relatives. Favour requires gratitude in return. Today we help

him, in future days he helps us. It may not be proper in the
whole process. But it is necessary.'

Ngoen tam nam or commission fees. Within the old *sakdina* administrative system, it was often customary for merchants to pay
commission fees or *kan jim kong* to their official patrons. The conventional rate was 10 per cent.

The modern bureaucracy has kept up this practice. It is
widely known that officials extract commissions from contractors
and suppliers on many kinds of expenditure ranging from
construction contracts to arms purchases.

A small number believe that such commission fees are a gift
of good will, a customary part of dealing with government
officials, and hence an integral part of the cost of doing business
with the government. Most, however, recognize that the practice
is clearly wrong. A little less than half describe it as bribery, and
over a third call it corruption.

When a businessman gives a commission fee to government department
or high government officials looking after a project, what do you call it?

		Per cent
a)	Gift of good will (*sin nam jai*)	16.1
b)	Part of the cost of the project	9.2
c)	Bribery	44.9
d)	The official is dishonest in his work	18.3
e)	Corruption	34.4
f)	Not corruption	3.5
g)	Not sure	6.8
h)	No answers, others	7.9

Many of those who find such commission fees acceptable
come from the groups of officials and businessmen involved in
the transactions. Some 34.4 per cent of businessmen and 37.2 per
cent of officials rate commission fees as gifts of good will or *sin
nam jai*. The businessmen are more ready than others to accept
commission fees as part of the cost of doing business. On enquiry,
they argue that it is simply the 'normal state of affairs'. Some say
that it is 'giving for compassion' (*hai douy khwam saneha*),

'welfare', or 'skimming off' (*hua queue*). Such terminology denotes the normal practice which businessmen are familiar with in dealing with government offices.

Outside the ranks of businessmen and officials, by far the majority see commission fees as 'dishonest', 'bribery' or 'corruption'. There are several reasons why commission fees on government expenditures draw such a critical response. First, this practice raises the total cost of the contract, or means that the quality of the goods supplied is lower. A businessman working in construction said: 'Assume the government has a budget to build 10 km of a road. If there is a commission fee of 10 per cent, that whole 10 km cannot be built. Or the quality will be lower. The construction contractor must calculate the commission fee and include it in the cost from the beginning.' Second, it is improper for an official to make private gain from public money. According to an MP: 'Anything that grows out of government money remains the public money. It must all be returned to the government.'

While most people consider *ngoen tam nam* or commission fees as corruption, they are prepared to modify their attitude in view of the way that the money is used. A business executive said: 'Commission fees are not always bad. It is not corruption if it can be used to improve the work performance of the section.' Similarly it may be acceptable if the proceeds are devoted towards increasing the welfare of all members of the department or section. Such answers implicitly rationalize that commission fees may be acceptable as a supplement to the low pay of government officials.

If a high military officers receives a commission fee on arms purchases, what do you call it?	
	Per cent
a) Improper behaviour	40.0
b) Dishonesty in duty	36.9
c) Corruption	52.8
d) Not corruption	5.0
e) No answers	12.5

People appear to be significantly more critical of commissions on arms purchases than on the previous example of commissions on government construction and supply contracts. The proportion rating the practice as corruption rises to over half. This critical attitude is shared by most of the sub-samples including middle class occupations, businessmen, workers, government officials and politicians.

An army colonel argued that commissions on arms purchases were not corruption but were gifts of good will or special discounts from the arms company. Moreover, he pointed out that the proceeds were often invested in welfare and used to build the bonds of loyalty between officers and men. He contended that such payments were not corruption because they made the army function more effectively.

Nepotism for the advancement of subordinates. In the old *sakdina* administrative system, promotions depended more on blood relations, social standing, personal loyalty and personal favours rather than merit. Again, elements of such practices have been carried over into the modern bureaucracy.

If a person is promoted because he is the blood relation or protégé of a senior officer, what do you call it?

		Per cent
a)	Inefficient administration	58.9
b)	Improper behaviour	47.6
c)	Dishonesty in duty	20.9
d)	Corruption	7.8
e)	Not corruption	3.7
f)	No answer, others	9.2

Most people recognize that official nepotism amounts to inefficient administration (*kan borihan ngan mai mi khunaphap*), but only a small number feel it merits the term corruption. Instead they use milder terms such as dishonesty or improper behaviour. On probing, they see nepotistic appointments as 'customary practice' and the results of 'personal compassion', but they also condemn them as 'favouritism', 'abuse of position', 'improper use of power', 'not being loyal to their office', and 'selfish'. They feel nepotism shows a 'lack of moral stand on the part of the boss'.

Those who accept nepotism often argue that there is nothing wrong with helping one's family of friends. A businessman said: 'If you don't help your relatives, who would you help?' Besides, such nepotism is also common in business circles, particularly in family-based firms. Some go further and rationalize that nepotism may enable someone with ability to advance very quickly. A businessman said: 'If one does not pay attention to capability, then this practice is most dangerous. But if the boss supports those of his subordinates who are capable, I do not think this is wrong. But if the person who gets promoted does nothing except look after the interests of his boss, this is very bad.'

People who have a more negative attitude towards nepotism contend that it makes those without connections lose heart and lose interest in working. The bureaucratic system will not be able to recruit capable people and it will become weaker over the years. A journalist from Chiang Mai said: 'I do not think it is right. It reduces the chances for promotion of other officials. They have no incentives to work. The whole system fails.' Another businessman said: 'I do not call it corruption, but it is bad for the civil service system. The government will get only people with no ability. This is no good, very damaging.'

Among the sub-sample of government officials, very few rated nepotism as corrupt or dishonest. In other words there appears to be a high level of acceptance of the practice among government officials, and especially among the military. This was confirmed in the focus groups and interviews. Officials tended to accept that patronage and nepotism in appointments was simply a customary prerogative of seniority. They would like to see the practice changed, but they recognized that at present it was deeply embedded in the operating practice of the bureaucracy. One official said:

'It is very difficult to tackle this problem. It is not really corruption. But it is not right. Work performance should be the criterion more than personal relations. But it depends whether the superiors have a moral stand. Subordinates cannot criticise them. They have to sit quiet. If they speak out, this would turn against them. So most keep their mouth shut.'

The small number who do see nepotistic appointments as corruption believe that the practice makes it difficult for the government to attract and retain capable recruits, with long-term consequences for the administrative system and for society as a whole.

Corruption in terms of time. Some senior officials make a point of arriving at work late and leaving early as a display of their senior status. In other cases, officials who have sideline business interests may use their official working time on these private affairs. These habits have been carried over from the traditional bureaucracy where senior officials did not expect to be called to public account.

If government officials go to work late, return home early, use official hours for private affairs, what do you call this?

		Per cent
a)	Improper behaviour	59.9
b)	Dishonesty in duty	39.8
c)	Corruption	17.3
d)	Not corruption	3.3
e)	No answers, others	9.6

If government officials misuse working time, most consider this improper behaviour, and hence not very serious. However, as many as two-fifths label such practice as dishonest, and 17.3 per cent call it corruption. Those who consider it more serious include the urban poor, farmers, middle class, workers, civil servants and politicians. On probing, they describe such misuse of official time as 'irresponsible', 'damaging to the civil service system', 'causing people loss of time and opportunity', 'a breach of duty'. A slum dweller called it corruption because such officials 'work part time but receive money on a full time basis'.

However, some point out that we cannot consider all the cases of officials arriving late and returning home early as corruption. We must look into the intention, the necessity of the individual concerned. A high-ranking police officer who considered this practice not as corruption but 'lack of discipline' expressed his sympathy for government officials as follows:

> 'This practice of using public time to do private things is very widespread in Thai society. I found it to be associated with low salary... Officials do not earn enough to maintain their livelihood... Sometimes they have to do sideline jobs... It should not be called corruption. They have to do it for survival.'

Political corruption

To examine attitudes towards corruption in the acquisition and use of political offices, we asked three questions about specific incidents in the recent past.

After the coup in 1991, the NPKC reconstituted the senate by appointment. General Sunthorn Kongsompong, the chairman of the NPKC, explained that they selected senators on the basis that they were close associates of the NPKC. He argued that these people were 'closest friends who have gone through thick and thin with them' (*phuen ruem tai*) during the seizure of power from Chatichai Choonhawan.

In making appointments to the senate, the NPKC chose people who were close to them personally. What do you call this?

	Per cent
a) Moral corruption	37.9
b) Political pay-off	28.9
c) Uncertain, cannot say	15.4
d) Not corruption	4.0
d) No answer, others	28.3

The sample was fairly evenly divided between those who considered such personal use of power as moral corruption (*kan khorrapchan thang sin tham*), those who judged it as a political pay-off, and those who could venture no opinion.

On probing, several different reasons were given for describing such appointments as moral corruption. First, the practice shows the attempt of the NPKC and their associates in business, politics and the bureaucracy to consolidate their grip on power for mutual gain. The senate appointments were used as reward for help in the coup, and as a means to strengthen political ties. Second, the appointments contradicted the principles of democracy. The NPKC tried to impose dictatorial rule by concentrating power among those close to them. Third, the choice of senators had no sound basis. It was not based on any consideration of quality or capability, and hence it was damaging for society as a whole.

Among those who rated these appointments as political pay-off, several used this description in a negative way and differed little in attitude from those rating it as moral corruption. They believed such appointments represented backward behaviour which was damaging to society as a whole.

Others, however, argued that such political pay-offs were a legitimate and functional element of the political system. The NPKC chose its friends because they wanted people with whom they would be able to work smoothly and effectively. A high-ranking police officer said: 'It is normal behaviour which has been done so often it has become the customary practice of those who seize power. They have to choose people who went through

If politicians distribute money during election time, what do you call it?	
	Per cent
a) Vote buying	91.6
b) Improper behaviour	27.5
c) Corruption	8.6
d) Not corruption	1.6
e) No answer, others	5.3

thick and thin with them. And this behaviour is not unlawful as the NPKC had already passed a law in support of their action.'

The majority of the sample viewed the practice of distributing money and gifts before elections as 'vote buying', but they do not call it corruption. Almost a third use the term 'improper behaviour'. The overall conclusion is that people treat vote buying with a degree of resigned acceptance. On probing, the rationale emerges as similar to the examples of payments offered to government officials. The politicians are willing to give. It is an act of 'giving with compassion', a gift of good will or *sin nam jai*. It is paid for people to go and vote for them on election day. It is bribery of a sort, but it is not binding on the receiver who can still take gifts from many candidates and vote however he likes.

Moreover, the term corruption is felt to apply more appropriately to people who already have power and use it wrongly. In the case of vote buying, the candidate does not yet have an official position to abuse. Besides, the money employed is not public money. Politicians will be accused of corruption only when they are holding an official post in the government and use their powerful positions to advance their personal interests. Buying votes may lead to corruption at a later stage, but it is not of itself corruption.

However, some respondents take a stronger attitude. One NGO worker called this 'the beginning of corruption', and another stated: 'We have to see the candidate's other behaviour. If he has so much money to distribute to people, he must expect to be a cabinet member, so that he can recoup the money back from abusing his position. It is clearly corruption.' Yet another NGO member said, 'This practice of vote buying is binding on the villager. Once a villager has accepted the money, he will vote for the giver to fulfil the obligation. This is a cultural practice among villagers. Once they are elected and installed in cabinet posts, politicians recoup their costs by corruption. So it is corruption through and through.'

A small businessman also thought this was 'definitely corruption. The candidate has already made his plan. Anyone putting up that much money must expect political payback. His

objective is not simply to be a good politician. The person's intention is definitely corrupt. He buys votes to lead people astray.'

If people donate gift cheques to politicians, how do you call it?	
	Per cent
a) Corruption	39.9
b) A cost of doing business	21.5
c) Gift of good will (*sin nam jai*)	18.2
d) Unsure, cannot say	17.5
e) Customary payment of respect to big people	7.3
f) Not corruption	4.1
g) No answer, others	16.2

The NPKC cited the corruption of the Chatichai cabinet as a
major reason for the coup in February 1991. Following the coup,
they set up a commission to investigate improper earnings by
ministers and their associates. This commission uncovered
examples of gift cheques for large amounts presented to the
ministers. Following the commission's findings, several ministers
had their assets seized on the grounds of having become
'unusually wealthy' from public office.

As in the previous example, the sample was starkly divided
between those who saw such gift cheques as clear examples of
corruption, and those who rationalized them as gifts of good will,
customary tokens of respect for important people, and part of the
cost of doing business. Also as in the previous example, a
significant number withheld any opinion.

Almost two-fifths classified the donation of gift cheques to
politicians as corruption. They explained that the sums involved
were very large, and were clearly paid in return for favours
performed by the politicians concerned. These sums of millions of
baht were not gifts out of love or respect, but were essentially
business transactions. A businessman stated: 'No businessman
gives free money. He must expect something in return. there is a
hidden intention.' A media professional said: 'I look at the
intention. A businessman presents gift cheques to politicians

because he expects a payback some time in the near future. He intends to receive something in return.' A military officer added: 'It is corruption because the giver must have some intention. Even though he may say he gives because of compassion, he knows what he will get in return. Giving in advance to secure a payback in the future is also corruption.'

However, around a fifth of the sample called such donations merely a gift of good will, and another fifth stated that they were simply a cost of doing business. Those who deny that such payments deserve to be called corruption rationalize this in two ways. Some say that it is rather 'giving out of compassion; well, it is also corruption, but with a difference'. Others say that we cannot presume that there is corruption involved unless we can prove that the giver has received any benefit.

Corruption and democracy

In the final section, we asked respondents which government offices and political parties they perceived to be most corrupt; whether corruption was more prevalent under dictatorial or democratic regimes; and what expectations they had for the trends of corruption in the future.

Many people perceive that the Ministry of Interior and its constituent departments are most associated with corruption. The Ministry itself ranked third among the top ten, while the Police Department within the same Ministry came first, and the Land and Customs Departments within the Ministry also ranked in the top ten. The poor perception of the Ministry of Interior spreads across all the different occupational sub-samples in the survey.

These findings were later corroborated by a public poll commissioned by the Ministry of Interior in November 1993 about what people think of the Ministry. The *Bangkok Post* (9 June 1994) reported a Ministry official saying that the results of the poll were suppressed 'because of the poor image of the Ministry in the eyes of the public and for fear the Ministry's reputation would be further tarnished'. According to the *Bangkok Post*: 'Most of those questioned in the survey said the Interior Ministry was the least honest and unjust [sic] government agency. The police were criticized as being impolite and acting arrogantly towards the ordinary person.... The Police Department received the lowest marks among Interior agencies.'

Even though secrecy makes it very difficult to find proof of corruption in the Ministry of Defence and the armed forces, the Ministry of Defence was ranked second after the Ministry of Interior. Among the middle class respondents, as many as 41.7 per cent perceived the Ministry of Defence as corrupt.

Thinking of corruption, what government offices do you think of most?

	Per cent
1) Police Department	33.7
2) Ministry of Defence	27.0
3) Ministry of Interior	26.0
4) Department of Transport	22.5
5) Land Department	10.1
6) Ministry of Commerce	7.6
7) Ministry of Agriculture	7.0
8) Ministry of Industry	3.8
9) Ministry of Finance	2.4
10) Customs Office	1.9

In the perceptions of corruption among political parties, two parties dominated: Chart Thai and Social Action. This view was shared fairly evenly across the occupational sub-samples. Over the next-ranked parties, there was more disagreement. Businessmen tended to rank Prachakon Thai third; politicians chose Chart Pattana; the middle class, civil servants, military, police officers, and workers chose Samakkhitham; farmers and the urban poor picked New Aspiration.

Thinking of corruption what political party do you think of?

		Per cent
1)	Chart Thai	53.5
2)	Social Action	37.9
3)	Samakkhitham	18.5
4=)	Prachakon Thai	9.5
4=)	New Aspiration	9.5
6)	Democrat	4.9
7)	Muan Chon/Rassadorn	3.1
8)	Palang Tham/Ekaparp	2.8
9)	Chart Pattana	2.6

Over half of the respondents could or would not venture an opinion on whether an elected government or military-dominated government was more corrupt. Among those who did have an opinion, the answers were almost equally divided.

Which type of government is more corrupt, an elected government or a military-dominated government?

		Per cent
a)	Elected government	22.2
b)	Military-dominated government	23.0
c)	Not sure, cannot say	34.2
d)	No answer	13.3
e)	Others	7.3

In the focus groups, those who could not choose explained their position. First, whether a government is corrupt or otherwise may have nothing to do with whether it results from an election or not. The important thing is whether the people who form the cabinet are honest. Second, most governments are selfish and all types are equally corrupt. Some respondents suggested that while a democratically elected government may start off well, as time goes on and as more information is revealed, it is often found that corruption is rampant.

Third, some respondents argued that at present we cannot say that political parties and MPs are real representatives of the people. They are simply a group of people who enter politics to seek benefits for themselves, their relatives and their friends. They are similar to the military juntas which seize power to obtain benefits for their group. Fourth, some felt that the procedure for investigating corruption among politicians and bureaucrats is not good enough to enable us to make a proper judgement.

Among the sub-samples, the proportion rating a military government as more likely to be corrupt than an elected government is higher among politicians and among middle class groups. In the focus groups, those with this opinion offered several arguments. First, an elected government is subject to different types of checks and balances (opposition parties, media, extra-parliamentary forces) which are absent under a military regime. A civil servant observed that at least under a democratic system people have more chance to scrutinize the government due to the openness of the media. In Thailand in the dictatorial regime under prime minister Sarit Thanarat, the media was not so free. Power was so concentrated that the prime minister could amass huge wealth through corruption without the public at large having any knowledge of it. The truth was revealed only after his death. According to this respondent, 'Under a dictatorial regime people cannot talk much for fear of being shot dead. But the government is corrupt all the same'.

Second, a dictatorial government survives through patronage and nepotism, and much less because of people's support. As a result, military regimes have a strong tendency to use corrupt means to seek benefits for their followers. Third, a dictatorial regime comes to power by force, and it thus pays less attention to the moral or legal basis of its rule. Fourth, members of non-elected governments are usually appointed from the ranks of permanent bureaucrats who are already familiar with methods of corruption.

Among respondents from the military, police and civil bureaucracy, 25.5 per cent felt an elected government was more likely to be corrupt as against 18.7 per cent for a military regime. First, they felt that senior bureaucrats who are well versed in bureaucratic rules and regulations will not engage in corruption. Second, government that comes from an election must pay a lot of money for the election campaign, and will need to recoup the investment by corruption in office. Third, politicians enter politics with an intention to make money. Fourth, once in power politicians tend to believe they can disobey rules and regulations with impunity. Fifth, politicians who have a business background enter politics to use it to advance their business.

While talking about elected governments being more corrupt, respondents from the bureaucracy often cited the case of the government led by prime minister Chatichai. And when referring to non-elected governments which are not corrupt, they cited the ministries under Prem and Anand. A police officer related that while Chatichai was prime minister, his superior who was a police colonel wanted to secure a promotion. He was recommended to approach a minister:

> 'When my boss came back from seeing the minister he shook his head and said "no go". The minister had demanded ten million baht. He had even suggested to my boss how to get this ten million baht. He told my boss to find ten merchants who were prepared to pay one million baht each. If my boss could thus obtain 10 million baht for the minister's party, then he would get his promotion.'

What do you expect will be the future trend of corruption among politicians and bureaucrats over the next 3-4 years?	Per cent
On the increase among bureaucrats	43.6
Stable/no change	4.5
On the decline among bureaucrats	8.2
Not sure	33.4
On the increase among politicians	44.6
Stable/no change	4.4
On the decline among politicians	10.1
Not sure	29.6

In the case of both politicians and officials, more people expected corruption to rise than decline in the future. The expectations concerning politicians and bureaucrats were not significantly different.

All occupational groups, except regular government officials, believe that corruption among bureaucrats will increase. Similarly all occupational groups other than politicians believe that corruption among politicians will increase.

In the focus groups, several reasons were given for this generally pessimistic assessment of the future trend of corruption. First, the democratic system in Thailand is not yet stable. Most Thai people still lack faith in democracy. Therefore the military can still intervene in politics at any time, and military regimes tend to engender corruption and allow the regular bureaucrats to engage in corruption as well.

Second, corruption has become institutionalized in the bureaucracy and will not easily be removed. Officials are used to it. Few can resist the social pressures to conform to established ways. Third, many government officials earn low salaries, and experience pressure to enhance their official earnings. Economic development increases the trends towards materialism and consumerism. Officials who live beyond their means will tend to satisfy their material wants by engaging in corruption.

Fourth, so far no government has really attempted to stem the cause of corruption among bureaucrats and politicians, such as by tightening up the anti-corruption laws. Fifth, the majority of the Thai people are still poor, and thus are unlikely to resist the practice of vote-buying. Sixth, many politicians still see politics as a means to become rich. Many MPs have become visibly richer since entering politics.

Seventh, the present political system still revolves around the issue of power seeking. Nepotism and patronage are still strong, and money remains the key to power. Eighth, new economic opportunities enable both politicians and bureaucrats to open up new avenues for corruption. Lastly, in recent years many of the businessmen who were previously involved in corruption with bureaucrats are now entering politics directly. Because of their experiences, they are resourceful in finding new ways to make money and to advance their business interests through the political system.

Respondents who are less certain about the future trend of corruption point to several factors which could lead the trend in different directions. First, it depends on the personality of the prime minister. If a good person becomes a prime minister then corruption may be lowered, and vice versa. Second, it depends on whether the future government has strong intention to solve corruption problems. Third, Thai politics is still prone to military coups. If there is a coup, corruption will increase. A democratic government may try to reduce corruption.

Fourth, it depends on whether the core party which forms the government is dominated by businessmen. If it is, then corruption will increase. Fifth, it depends on the economic prospects of the country. Better economic prospects are likely to reduce corruption as incomes increase. Sixth, it also depends on whether the parliamentary opposition can provide an effective countercheck to reduce corruption. Seventh, the NPKC's seizure of the Chatichai cabinet ministers' assets has caused a great deal of shame and loss of face which may act as a disincentive to future ministers.

The small percentage of respondents who think corruption will decline in the future are optimistic that democracy in Thailand will grow stronger, transparency in information and decision-making processes will increase, and the counter balancing forces outside the parliament will also help to monitor the performance of the elected government. Moreover, politicians should learn a lesson from the NPKC seizure of power. If they continue to be corrupt, the military will find a cause to seize power again. Politicians should try to avoid presenting the military with such an opportunity. Finally, with higher incomes and higher education as well as more open media, people should progress quickly and learn not to sell their votes. The continuous improvement in salaries and welfare provisions of government officials will help them to be less corrupt.

Conclusion

A section of the Thai population including a portion of the bureaucracy is conscious of the fact that under a system of modern public administration bureaucrats and politicians are 'public persons' working in 'public organizations' with the function of providing 'public services'. But there are still other segments of people and bureaucrats who do not share this view. Those who appreciate the concept of 'public office' are distributed across all occupational groups but are significantly more common among NGO workers, academics, media people and other professionals. Those who do not appreciate the concept of public services are also distributed widely across society, but they tend to be concentrated among the military, police, civil servants and the lower echelons of society, namely farmers and slum dwellers. Therefore the misinterpretation of the functions of the public administration system is not confined to any one occupational group. Any attempt to correct this view must be done at the national level, so that society as a whole undergoes the same learning process.

Many Thais still see corruption simply in terms of *kan chor rat bang luang* or the old concept of 'cheating from the people and cheating from the royal coffer'. They still see bribes given to officials as being *sin nam jai* or gifts of good will, which are acceptable or tolerable. At the same time, officials rationalize that since they do not request the bribes overtly, there is no moral or social wrong incurred in receiving gifts which are 'willingly' presented to them. The giving and receiving of bribes in this way is considered a 'mutual transaction' between two individuals. It therefore creates no damage to anyone else, or to the society at large. In short, the transaction is acceptable as it is done in the context of *khwam mi nam jai* or generosity, which is upheld as a good thing under the social value system.

The majority of respondents feel that palm-greasing or giving tea money to quicken up official procedures is normal and acceptable. They consider it a 'wrong thing' which government officials should not do, but they judge that the offence is not so serious. The officials do not ask for the money. The giver is willing. The individual sums are small. The giver buys convenience.

Only a minority apply the negative terms of 'extortion' or 'corruption' to such practices. The definition of 'cheating the people' is interpreted very flexibly among the Thai public. It is conditional (on scale, intention, social context) and not straightforward. The old rationale of the public administration under *sakdina* is still influential in the consciousness and thinking of Thai people on this issue. It is stronger than the new concept of public office.

The principles underlying the definition of 'cheating from the royal coffer' are similar to those underlying 'cheating the people'. Many do not mind government officials taking little things from the office to be used at home. They understand that such behaviour is improper, but they do not consider it a serious offence. However, they mind rather more if officials use government cars and petrol for personal use, to the point of calling it corruption. The difference appears to be largely the *value* of the articles involved. Pencils are cheap. Cars are not.

In short, for many Thais acts of 'cheating the people' and 'cheating from the royal coffer' will be called corruption only if they involve large sums of money, stem from aggressively greedy intentions, and have consequences which are clearly damaging for society as a whole. Therefore *chor rat bang luang* as a concept is narrower than 'corruption' in English, which covers all manner of behaviour with much less conditionality with respect to value, intention, and social consequence.

The concept that officials and politicians are public servants is not at all widely accepted. In many respects, the codes of conduct of the old *sakdina* bureaucracy have been carried over into the present. It is still considered acceptable to use high official position to make money, to reward friends, and to demand special personal privileges.

It is common for high-ranking bureaucrats, military and police officers to use their powerful positions to provide protection to businessmen. For over half a century, military leaders have occupied posts as chairmen, board members or advisors of private companies. Military officers argue that this is a long-standing customary practice which in no way contravenes the law.

The majority of our sample respondents feel this practice is 'improper' but not a serious offence. In effect, society still condones this practice and hence encourages the development of 'political soldiers' and 'business soldiers', with consequent damage for norms and principles of professionalism in the civilian bureaucracy and armed forces.

The political crises in October 1973 and May 1992 both disrupted the relationships between soldiers and businessmen. However, the effect in 1973 was only temporary and may prove so again in the 1990s. If the Thai public does not demand higher standards of behaviour in line with the concept of public office, then the military will find ways to resume their old habits.

Commission fees or *ngoen tam nam* are the basis of a large black economy which permeates the bureaucracy. It is a well-known fact that a large number of high-ranking bureaucrats receive regular extra income from commission fees levied from the purchase of equipment, arms deals, construction contracts, and other forms of government expenditure. An MP who was several times member of the budget scrutinizing committee estimated that the leakage out of the government budget for the purchase of equipment and building of infrastructure due to commission fees is in the order of 30-40 per cent. Bureaucrats see commission fees as 'part of normal business practices'. In effect, they interpret their own role as salesmen rather than as public servants.

Among professionals and other middle class occupations, there is a higher-than-average appreciation of the proper duties of public servants. Among the lower echelons of society, there appears to be a significant sensitivity to forms of corruption which involve large sums of money and which incur obvious social damage. These two social groups may form the basis for more concerted pressure to reform the practices of politicians and bureaucrats. At present, however, this pressure remains weak. Politicians and bureaucrats can still rely on the fact that the majority have a poorly developed conception of 'public office', a resigned acceptance of many forms of abuse of power, and an ingrained deference towards political and administrative position.

Ever since 1947, military dictators have cited corruption and maladministration as reasons for overthrowing representative governments. To assist the future of democracy, elected governments should campaign for the public to understand the issue of corruption, so that they may begin to act as a more effective countercheck. The elected government must have the will to reform the public administration and to decentralize power, so that the public administration works truly for the benefit of the people. Political parties must develop towards becoming public organizations which people can control, monitor, and trust in order that they may be in a position to initiate change towards a firmer, more stable, and more just democracy.

Notes.

1. These are: (1) businessman and executives (managing directors, deputy managing director, major shareholders); (2) businessmen with small and medium sized operations; (3) politicians (MPs, members of provincial councils, members of municipalities); (4) university academics; (5) media persons (6) students; (7) NGO workers; (8) professionals (doctors, engineers, architects, managers, directors of companies who are non-owners); (9) civilian government officials; (10) military officers; (11) police; (12) white collar workers; (13) blue collar workers; (14) state enterprise workers; (15) vendors; (16) housewives in slums; (17) hired labourers (taxi drivers, barbers, general labourers); (18) farmers (rice farmers, cash crop growers, fruit tree growers, fishermen) and (19) village headmen, *tambon* headmen.

2. For details of the answers for all the questions, by sex and occupations, the reader is requested to consult the Thai version which is a full report of this same study. The book is entitled *Khorrapchan kap prachathippatai thai* [Corruption and Thai Democracy], by Pasuk Phongpaichit and Sungsidh Piriyarangsan, published by the Political Economy Centre, Faculty of Economics, Chulalongkorn University, Bangkok, 1994.

6
CAUSES AND CURES

How do people define corruption? Do they see corruption as a major contemporary problem? If so, how do they think the problem may be overcome? We investigated the views of people of different walks of life through interviews, a series of 85 focus groups held between March and June 1992, and five workshops held in May-June 1993 (the same research programme referred to in the previous chapter). In this chapter, we summarize and present people's opinions on the definition of corruption, on its causes, and on the methods to control it.

Corruption and *sin nam jai*

Nam jai or 'good will from the heart' is highly valued as a personal attribute in Thai culture. The term *sin nam jai* or a 'gift of good will' is usually applied to gifts given in return for a favour done by a friend, relative, acquaintance, or official. Such goodwill gifts are also viewed highly positively in Thai culture. Gifts to government officials in return for a favour or service rendered may be seen as *sin nam jai* (positive) or corruption (negative) depending on the particular cultural perspective adopted. Within a modern concept of the role of bureaucracy, they constitute corruption. Within a traditional Thai context of relations between rulers and ruled, they may be assimilated into *sin nam jai*. This overlap complicates the process of defining corruption, and that of devising means to reduce or eliminate it.

When Thai people go to a government office for any kind of public service and are satisfied with the service they receive, they like to show their appreciation. For many people just saying thank you is not enough. They like also like to offer gifts or money. Popular gifts for this purpose include flowers, Buddha images, liquor, handkerchiefs, soap, pens, clocks, watches, dolls. Gifts offered in this way are called *sin nam jai*. This *sin nam jai* may also take the form of an invitation to a good restaurant, or a gift of money to be used for the welfare of all officials in the section or department.

Attempts to eliminate corruption touch directly on the set of beliefs and everyday ritualistic relationships between an ordinary person and an official. To challenge corruption, it will first be necessary to challenge the concept of *sin nam jai* in the specific context of the relationships between rulers and ruled. Without such a challenge, the modern conception of public office cannot take root.

Criteria for separating *sin nam jai* and corruption. Most people covered in our study think that to qualify as *sin nam jai*, gifts should be 'things' rather than money. They should be 'things' of small value because gifts of things with high value come close to being a bribe. A Songkhla MP said: 'If a Benz car is given as a gift to an official, this is definitely corruption. But if a gift of small value is given, it may be regarded as a gift of good will.' If businessmen give land, a car, or large sums of money to government officials or ministers, for most people this cannot be considered as *sin nam jai*. A Khon Kaen MP said: 'Giving a small amount of money like 10-100 baht may pass as *sin nam jai*, but not when it involves hundreds of thousands of baht'.

The conclusion that *sin nam jai* should be 'things' more than money, and small rather than large in value, reflects the perception that 'corruption' is a form of behaviour which seeks to reap large profits with serious impact on society. A businessman said: 'In fact even one baht is corruption. But nowadays when people talk about corruption we think of big, serious things. Thus the word corruption is now associated with a large amount of money or things of great value.'

How then is the value of *sin nam jai* measured? What distinguishes a small, acceptable amount from a large, corrupt amount?

The valuation of *sin nam jai* is variously determined by the income, occupation, and social status of the donor and recipient, by the nature of the personal relationship between them, by the extent of mutual interests, and by their personal preferences and intentions. Businessmen think the valuation of *sin nam jai* depends on the status and ranks of the giver and the receiver. Although they agree with the principle that *sin nam jai* should have only moderate value, they may believe it quite acceptable to present a Benz car as *sin nam jai* as long as the giver is willing and he can afford it. For a businessman, value is always relative.

One businessman respondent argued that the valuation of *sin nam jai* is determined by the personal relationship between the giver and the receiver. If they are very close and there is much mutual business interest, then a gift of significant monetary value may still qualify as *sin nam jai*. Another businessman talked about giving *sin nam jai* to influential high-ranking officers on such occasions as a birthday or the new year in this way: 'If that officer is highly respected, without having anything to do with business interests, that officer will receive things like a vase of flowers. But officers who are important because of business interests will receive gifts of much higher value.'

People in professional occupations think that the valuation of *sin nam jai* is determined by the value of the services or work which the donor requires from the recipient. If the value of the work to the donor is high, then a gift of high value is acceptable as *sin nam jai*. However, there should be a ceiling to this value, otherwise it qualifies as a bribe rather than a gift of good will. Some businessmen also think there should be standard criteria for *sin nam jai*. For instance they say a commission fee of 5-10 per cent of the total value of a construction project is a natural or normal price. If an official asks for a commission above this 'market rate', they will regard this as corruption or extortion. In other words for businessmen the price of *sin nam jai* should be determined by them, not by the officials. By this reasoning businessmen can give less if they are not so wealthy, and more if they are wealthy enough to afford it.

The capacity to pay is one of the criteria. It is also a matter of giving willingly and giving with 'compassion'. According to Thai law, a person can give any amount of money to a government officer, provided the giving is done for reasons of personal compassion on the part of the giver. This reasoning can be used to counter accusations of corruption in the court of law. Obviously the reasoning or the thinking of businessmen is no doubt influenced by this legal aspect. These various conditions give businessmen a high degree of flexibility in determining what may be classified as *sin nam jai*.

People with lower economic status than businessmen and professionals, namely, the urban poor and farmers, do not think there should be a ceiling to *sin nam jai*. There should be no limit to personal willingness or good will. A village headman from Chiang Mai said: 'The more or less of this *sin nam jai* cannot be set by a restricted amount of money. It depends on the willingness of the giver.' A *tambon* headman in Lopburi said that '*sin nam jai* may amount to 10 million or 100 million baht'. A village headman from Lopburi said: 'It can be any amount depending on what the person can afford. If the giver likes to give, so be it. This is the meaning of *sin nam jai.*'

The importance of intention. All occupational groups in our sample think that the intention of the giver and receiver is an important factor when assessing the difference between *sin nam jai* and corruption. For the transaction to be called *sin nam jai*, most respondents think that the intentions of the giver and receiver should correspond to certain general principles.

First, *sin nam jai* must be the result of the giver's wish to give, without any prior agreement or promises. If the official who is the receiver 'has made a request' beforehand, the transaction is considered corruption. A civil servant said: 'If the official asks, it is corruption as it forces the giver to give unwillingly. But in the case of *sin nam jai*, the giver gives willingly. The official has not asked.' The manager of an agro-products firm in Chiang Mai explained: 'We in the private sector sometimes would like to give

something to officials in return for the good cooperation we receive from them. In that case the transaction is not corruption. We
see it as *sin nam jai.*' The willingness to give is a function of the
donor's satisfaction with the services rendered by the official in
the past. Another manager said: 'From the point of view of the
giver, the transaction is *sin nam jai.* But an onlooker may say that
the official is corrupt. If the official worked to his full capacity
and we give him something, we can call that *sin nam jai.* But if the
official drags on the work, with expectation that we would give
him some money before he would finish the task, then it is
corruption.'

Second, *sin nam jai* must originate from the personal
preference or personal compassion (*hai duay khwam saneha*) of the
giver. *Sin nam jai* is something which the recipient does not expect
to receive beforehand. If the recipient has a prior expectation, and
expects to receive something in return for the service which is in
fact his regular duty, then the action qualifies as corruption. The
gift must take place after the work is done, because the giver is
happy with the services and would like to show appreciation. An
MP said: 'The term *sin nam jai* refers to a transaction in a situation
where a person comes to contact us for a service. Since we render
a good service and the person accomplishes his work, the person
feels like giving us something. It could be 500 baht or it could be a
gift of things. I would consider such a transaction as *sin nam jai.*'

While most respondents thought the term *sin nam jai* applies
only to gifts given after the transaction is complete, some of the
policemen in our sample thought the gift should occur before the
work is done. If it happens after, then it will be corruption. A
middle-ranking police officer said:

> 'I am speaking from the point of view of a government official. If
> it is *sin nam jai*, the giving must come first before the work is
> done. But if the giving occurs after the work is done, I am not
> sure that it can be called *sin nam jai.* I give you an example. One
> of my friends asks me to send my subordinates to help him with
> some tasks, such as organizing some errands for him. He then
> gives my subordinates a sum of money to pay for the cost of
> transport and food. There is some money left over and he gives

that to my subordinates too. I see that this is a case of *sin nam jai*. It is not that my subordinates specify that for the job done, there must be 500 baht or 1,000 baht. If that was the case, this will not be *sin nam jai*. But in the example, my friend has said that the money is for transport and food and what is left over my subordinates can have. I find this kind of case all the time in my area. But if the payment occurs after the work is done, then it points to corruption. Don't you agree? If the payment is made beforehand, the intention is clear, isn't it?'

Third, *sin nam jai* must be given without any condition attached, and the donor must not expect any future *quid pro quo*. An NGO worker said: '*Sin nam jai* is a transaction in which the giver does not want anything else in return. But corruption is a transaction which involves hidden motives and hidden vested interests.' In other words the intention of the giver is important. If the giver gives without expecting anything in return, then it is *sin nam jai*. If the giver expects something in return then it is corruption.

Fourth, the recipient must not deviate from rules and regulations as a result of the gift. He must not bend the rules or engage in immoral or dishonest behaviour. The donor must not expect anything irregular, anything beyond what the official may legitimately provide. If the gift results in some irregularity in return, then it qualifies as corruption and not as *sin nam jai*.

Fifth, most respondents believed that even bribes to speed up work and commission fees on construction projects could be classified as *sin nam jai* if the proceeds were used for the welfare of the whole department rather than for individual gain.

Finally, for some respondents almost any transaction may qualify as *sin nam jai* if it is freely contracted between both parties. The managing director of a company recounted:

'In the business world here in Bangkok, when we contact government officials, we cannot wait for them forever to take time to do their work. The correct government procedure is complicated and takes a long time. We cannot afford to wait. Therefore we ask if they have any problem. They say there will be no problem and that they will make sure the work gets done quickly. We consider then that what we give them is *sin nam jai* or the cost of their effort [*kha nuey*]. We think it is their right to receive because they cut corners for us especially.'

Most respondents consider gifts to powerful people on birthdays or New Year's Day are a customary way of paying respect to them as persons with seniority (*phu yai*). The gifts are part of *sin nam jai*. But *sin nam jai* may turn into bribery if the gift has too high a value, indicating a hidden intention between the giver and receiver; or if the gift is given in return for a favour anticipated or already done; or if the giving occurs outside any special occasion or outside the gift-giving season.

The boundary between *sin nam jai* and corruption. A segment of the middle class, especially among academics and the media, think that *sin nam jai* and corruption are the same thing. They argue this case on several grounds.

First, they are the same thing because they involve mutual interest between the giver and the receiver. According to a journalist:

'The words may be different but the actions have the same features, namely returning favours to people whom we know. The word *sin nam jai* entails quid pro quo. If the giver does not expect anything in return, he would not give. In the context of Thai society, when someone does things for us we do something for them in return. It is always a *quid pro quo*. When this applies to government officials, it is corruption.'

An academic observed that the linking of the words *sin* (asset, property, cash) with *nam jai* (good will) implied a transaction, an exchange of items of value:

'Whenever the word *sin* [asset] is connected to *nam jai* [good will], using *sin* in replace of *nam jai* or exchanging *sin* for *nam jai* or payment for other people's *nam jai*, this involves a valuation

of something, with expectations and consequences. The whole
thing is about valuation.'

Second, a transaction may be viewed by the giver and the
receiver as *sin nam jai*, but viewed from outside, it may be perceived as corruption. Another academic argued:

> 'Well, *sin nam jai* reflects only the view of the giver and the
> receiver with mutual interests even though they have not had a
> prior agreement or promise... But for outside people looking in,
> it is corruption, even though the giver and the receiver do not
> think of the word corruption and use *sin nam jai* instead. In fact
> the true meaning is the same.'

The practice of *sin nam jai*, in the context of transactions
between the public and government officials, brings out the
incongruence between the duty of an official as a public office
holder in a modernized public administration, and the traditional
concept of the 'good will' ordinary people owe to officials for the
performance of their duty. Many Thai people think it is legitimate
to give gifts and money to officials in return for their regular
duty. They rationalize this assessment in terms of traditional
values, customary relationships, special occasions, good intentions, acceptable values. This rationalization of *sin nam jai* is
widespread among all occupational groups, but is particularly
strong among businessmen, officials and the lowest income
categories. The lowest income groups of farmers and urban poor
accept the practice because they have little concept of the role of
modern public administration. Wealthy businessmen accept the
practice because they want to overcome the slow, costly and
complicated procedures of the public administration. But certain
segments of the middle class have begun to see that in the context
of public administration, *sin nam jai* and corruption are actually
the same thing.

Corruption, politics and society

All the occupational groups in our study agree that corruption has both good and bad points. But mostly the good points are for the individuals, while the bad aspects fall on the administration or on the society.

Several good aspects of corruption are mentioned. It can speed up the pace of economic growth. Corruption money reduces red tape, enabling more investment to take place, resulting in higher income and higher employment. The benefits of economic growth have a value in themselves even though ministers and officials receive corruption money as payments for their performance. Governments which are perceived to have achieved economic growth by this approach include those of Sarit (1957-63) and Chatichai (1988-91). A high-ranking air force officer said:

> 'If the government under Chatichai paid money to political parties but brought a lot of progress to the nation, we should not care about corruption. I see nothing wrong about General Sarit. Even though General Sarit was corrupt, he brought progress to the nation. How else would he feed his subordinates if he had no money.'

Some respondents pointed out that corruption provides incentives for bureaucrats to work harder, to serve the public better. Businessmen are especially happy that officials work faster when their palms are greased, because speed is important to their business. A businessman said: 'Well, it is altogether more convenient. We can go home earlier. We do not have to wait for the clearing of our goods two to three more days. This reduces our costs.'

On the negative side, some perceive that corruption has a moral cost as a result of the way in which it puts wealth in the pockets of individual bureaucrats, politicians and businessmen. Many also perceive that corruption has a high social cost, which occurs in several forms. First, official corruption has caused damage to the environment and public safety. Vast areas of the country's forests have been destroyed. Officials have allowed factories to release industrial waste into rivers, the sea and the air, resulting in pollution, environmental deterioration, and health risks. The resulting social costs in the form of bad health, medical care, pollution controls, and deterioration of public amenities are recognized as enormous. Corruption has also been the cause of sub-standard construction of factories, hotels and other buildings resulting in accidents, disasters, death and disability.

Second, the commission fees on government construction projects and purchases of materials and equipment cause the government each year extra expenditure to the tune of thousands of millions of baht, and often result in substandard facilities, accidents, and large repair bills. Third, corruption enables some businessmen to have special privileges, giving rise to situations of unfair competition. Corruption payments are absorbed as part of the cost of business operations, and in the end are passed on to consumers. Finally, corruption causes the public administration system to deteriorate. The public lose faith in it. Bureaucrats as individuals lose their dignity because of their own dishonesty.

Politicians or bureaucrats. Businessmen, politicians, most middle class groups and a segment of workers think that permanent officials are more corrupt than politicians. Bureaucrats, workers, the urban poor, farmers, and a minority of the middle class see politicians as more corrupt. The tendency is for well-educated and well-to-do people to view bureaucrats as more corrupt than politicians. But people with relatively low education and low income have a tendency to view politicians as more corrupt.

People who think bureaucrats have a tendency to be more corrupt contend that the Thai bureaucracy has great autonomy and hence a considerable capacity to demand corruption money. By contrast, politicians come and go with elections and their terms of office. They need the cooperation of permanent bureaucrats to carry out corruption successfully, as bureaucrats know the rules and regulations and their loopholes. Furthermore, investigating corruption among bureaucrats is more difficult than among politicians. This is especially so in the case of the Ministry of Defence. In addition, permanent bureaucrats stay in office longer than politicians, and hence are in a position to create syndicates among themselves. In some cases these syndicates become so powerful as to be like a state within a state. Many people in our study further argued that as bureaucrats are numerous and have to deal with ordinary people all the time, they have more opportunities to engage in corruption.

We further asked the focus group respondents to debate whether bureaucratic corruption was the result of the low moral standards of individual officers, the conflict between public administration and business systems, or the bureaucrat's misinterpretation of the role of a public office holders in a modern public administration system.

While many respondents lamented the greed and low moral standards of individual office holders, few pinned the blame on a collapse of moral standards. More pointed to the ingrained culture of the bureaucracy which sucks new recruits into its webs of syndicated corruption. In many cases high-ranking officials themselves are corrupt and do not set good examples for their subordinates. They protect their subordinates if they are found guilty of corruption. Some ministers use the excuse of national security to have their offices exempted from the rules and regulations on corruption.

Respondents also remarked on the impact of social norms and social constraints. Contemporary Thai society values material wealth with little consideration for its origin. Bureaucrats cannot legitimately make money as fast as businessmen. They resort to corruption in order to become wealthy and hence to acquire a high status in society. The society expects high-ranking officers to have the wealth to perform certain social functions, such as to provide donations for charitable organizations. Charity organizers ask them to donate money or to help sell tickets for charitable feasts and fairs. These high-ranking officials in turn ask their subordinates to sell the tickets for them. In our interviews with police officers, they talked about having been asked to sell charity tickets by their superiors all the time. If they cannot do it, their promotion prospects will suffer. So they ask for favours from businessmen, merchants and traders in their area. One favour must be returned by another favour. Businessmen are prepared to buy these charity tickets but they then expect the police to turn a blind eye to their illegal activities or to give them protection. This should not be blamed on the low moral standards of individual policemen alone. It must be seen in the context of social expectations, the high regard for wealth, the equation of wealth with power, and the incongruence between low official salaries and high expectations of official patronage.

In summary, while some people see corruption among bureaucrats as being caused by the low moral standards of individual bureaucrats, more people see it as a result of weaknesses in bureaucratic systems.

Many respondents also perceive that corruption among bureaucrats results from the conflict between public administration and business. Respondents from all social groups complained about the long and complicated procedures involved in the present system of public administration. Many also point to the lack of transparency in decision making, ranging from small everyday official transactions to major decisions on multi-million baht infrastructure projects and arms purchase deals. The lack of transparency and the complicated administrative procedures give opportunities for bureaucrats to 'sell speediness'. Whoever wants fast service must pay. After making cost-benefit analyses, many businessmen choose to pay rather than wait. There is thus a conflict between the system of administration which imposes complicated procedures and keeps decision-making processes secret, and the craving for speed, efficiency and transparency of the business sector. This conflict will persist as long as the bureaucracy is not reformed, and the conflict creates opportunities for corruption.

Most respondents agreed that part of the problem is that bureaucrats do not fully understand their roles as public office holders. Many people complain that bureaucrats have became so used to receiving tea money that they tend to go slow or refuse to perform their regular duties unless they are offered extra compensation. They are also prone to abuse their powerful positions, by making use of rules and regulations for private gain, or by taking advantage of loopholes in the laws to extort money from people.

The causes of political corruption. The respondents cited eight major causes of corruption among politicians. First, it is due to the personal weakness of individual politicians. Second, some enter politics in order to protect their business interests. Third, once in powerful positions they see the prospects of making money and cannot resist. Fourth, they are assisted in corrupt dealing by permanent bureaucrats. Fifth, they want to recoup the large expenditure they laid out during the election campaign. Sixth, their constituents demand all kinds of pay-offs for helping them win the elections, compelling the politicians to find financial resources in order to maintain their popular support into the future. Seventh, they are forced to find money for the political work of the party. Eighth, they need to repay merchants and businessmen who have helped them win the elections.

These eight factors may be reduced to three major causes: individual weakness, an amoral political system, and cooperation for mutual gains between politicians and bureaucrats. The majority of respondents focus on the second factor, the amoral political system.

Respondents believed that this amoral political system arises from the domination of political parties by merchants, local influential people (*jao pho*) and other businessmen. They sponsor the political parties and their electoral candidates. The parties work for the private gain of their sponsors rather than for the good of the society at large or even for the people who elect the party candidates. None of the existing political parties have started from grass roots support. Rather, they originated as interest groups of influential people and businessmen. At election time, they circumvent the democratic process by vote buying with the help of local influential men. New recruits of young politicians may begin their career with some idealistic fervour. But most later succumb to the situation and accept the practice of vote buying. Unless this amoral political system is changed, parliamentary politics will not attract recruits with a strong moral stand, and corruption among politicians will continue.

Cures for corruption

Our respondents perceived that bureaucratic corruption is caused both by the low moral standards of individual bureaucrats, by the deficiencies of the administrative system, and by the pressures and constraints which society imposes on officials. Any movement of reform must address all these causes. Attempts to improve the moral standards of individual officials alone will not strike at the root cause. Corruption is strongly ingrained in the society itself, hence any solution must begin at the level of society. There must be a movement within society to combat this problem on a large scale. People's consciousness and appreciation of the problems must be raised until popular opinion becomes a force pressuring the society and government to tackle the problem together. The respondents suggested two approaches.

First, one solution must begin with individuals' subjective perceptions of what is legitimate and what is corrupt. Attempts must be started to improve the standards of business, professional and official ethics through various institutions such as schools, professional clubs, business associations, and the individual household.

Second, some objective measures can be enforced through three major channels: political controls, administrative controls, and public controls.

Political controls should include systems of checks and balances built into the constitutional structure of the parliament, cabinet system, and other democratic institutions. It will be necessary to strengthen parliamentary scrutiny committees, establish an ombudsman, and improve the power, scope and efficiency of existing counter-corruption agencies such as the Office of Auditor General and the Counter Corruption Commission.

Administrative controls can be tightened by improving systems for budget scrutiny within government offices, reducing legal loopholes, and prescribing stricter standards of performance for government offices to act as a yardstick of efficiency. Systems to scrutinize department budgets in particular have not yet been effectively used to force corrupt government departments to reform. Laws to guarantee the freedom of the press and the other media also will help ensure transparency in decision-making processes on big public projects. Such laws will also help the public to become well-informed about government actions and decisions, and hence better equipped to impose social sanctions against corrupt officials and politicians.

Public controls should include well-known methods such as public hearings and public enquiries which are a common feature of democratic systems. The decentralization of public administration will also assist public monitoring of official activities.

Short-term controls on bureaucratic corruption. Respondents suggested short-term measures to improve the moral standards of officials and politicians. There should be a systematic campaign to make bureaucrats understand their roles as holders of public office, to increase their sense of public responsibility, and to make them aware of the damage which corruption can cause both to their own offices and to the society at large. There should be a campaign to make officials feel repelled by corruption. Officials should be encouraged to live within their means and to avoid gambling and other vices. These campaigns must be systematic and cover all levels of officials from low to high.

Respondents also suggested methods to correct weaknesses in bureaucratic systems. The salary of bureaucrats should be upgraded in accordance with the changes in the cost of living in order to reduce the tendency for low-income officials to accept gifts and bribes as income supplements. There should be an improvement in the existing rules and regulations for countering corruption, by making the rules clearer, simpler, but more effective. The government should make ordinary people become more aware of their rights to receive service from government offices so as to stop officials taking advantage of people's ignorance in order to make private gains for themselves. The practice of patronage and nepotism in official appointments and promotions must be replaced with systems based on merit.

The Counter Corruption Commission should be made more effective by giving it legal powers to impose penalties on officials found guilty of corruption. At present, the CCC only has the power to investigate a bureaucrat following a complaint. If the results of the investigation substantiate the corruption charges, the CCC can only report the case to the superior of the official accused. The superior of the accused will order a second investigation and then decide whether the case should be sent to the public prosecutor for criminal charges, or settled through disciplinary action within the department. Very often officers found suspect by the CCC get away with reprimands or departmental disciplinary action. Even if evidence points to criminal behaviour and the matter is sent to the public prosecutor, the public prosecutor will not use the evidence carefully collected and recorded by the CCC. It will begin its own fresh investigation. Past cases show that the public prosecutor often finds that there is not enough evidence to prosecute. This has happened time and again and the CCC has become very frustrated. It has been suggested therefore that the results of the investigation by the CCC should be used by the public prosecutor, so as to reduce duplication and make the control of corruption more effective. The argument against making the CCC more powerful is that its power may also corrupt. But there is no point in setting up a Counter Corruption Commission if its investigations always come to nothing.

Respondents also suggested that all high-ranking military and civilian officers should be made to declare their assets, and their income and expenditure accounts every three to five years. These balance sheets should be posted for the public to see. Purchase of high-value articles and assets must be reported and officials must be able to show where the purchase money comes from.

The government should pass an information act which will enable the public to have access to government information. Secret documents must have a lifespan, so that they become available to the public after a certain period of time.

Longer-term measures against bureaucratic corruption. In addition, respondents proposed more long-term measures designed to create standards of behaviour for officials, politicians, and the people at large, to promote a more moral political system, to decentralize public administration and to overcome the poverty problems which lie at the root of certain forms of corruption.

A long-term campaign should be mounted through the family and educational institutions to make corruption socially unacceptable behaviour, and to reduce the importance of materialism in the scale of social values.

There should be serious attempts to promote true democracy at the grass roots level. The highly centralized public administration system must be decentralized to permit more autonomy among smaller units and local communities. Decentralization may begin in those government departments which are perceived as the most corrupt, by allowing representatives of people in the locality to have power to investigate and review the work of these departments directly.

The whole bureaucracy should be made smaller but more efficient. By this means the government could afford to pay each officer more, could select a better calibre of people, and could have more confidence that recruitment and promotion are based on merit rather than nepotism.

Lastly, the government must seriously set about the task of eradicating poverty, improving income distribution, and providing better access to education. If the economic standards of the majority of the population are raised and income inequality is reduced, then corruption among certain groups of people can be expected to decline.

In sum, people believe that in order to reduce corruption among bureaucrats, the reform of the public administration system must go hand in hand with attempts to raise the consciousness and appreciation of the role of bureaucrats as public office holders. Corruption must be made more costly and more risky by tightening the rules and regulations, increasing penalties on all parties concerned, and improving enforcement. Bureaucratic efficiency should also be improved so that it no longer pays for a businessman to try to corrupt officers. A reformed public administration system must be able to give its members a sense of dignity, and a decent income commensurate with their status in society. It should be a system which values people who are honest, who understand their roles as public office holders, and who perform well for the public.

Combatting political corruption. To combat corruption among politicians, respondents suggested two major avenues: first strengthening the civil society so that it can eventually control the political system, and second creating more effective systems of checks and balances among politicians.

In order to strengthen the civil society, political parties and other institutions must provide political education to the people, through, for example, regular campaigns to make people become fully aware of their rights, the provision of legal education, and more effective campaigns against vote buying. Decentralization of public administration is also an important means to strengthen the civil society at the grass roots levels.

At the same time, the society must have mechanisms for investigating and controlling the work of ministers and MPs in the parliament. The media and other extra-parliamentary forces are important checks on politicians. In the policy decision-making process, representatives of different segments of the civil society, such as trade unions, professional associations, NGOs, representatives of slums and rural communities, should be permitted to play a more active role.

In order to create a self-scrutinizing system among politicians and a more moral political system, respondents said political parties will have to be reformed. They must become more accountable to a popular base, for their internal organization, their finances, and their policies. Political parties must cease to be merely extensions of business groups.

Politicians are also public office holders. They are public persons who are subject to scrutiny by the people and society at large. They should be honest and work with professionalism. Candidates with undesirable attributes and histories should not be allowed to run in the elections. At the moment there is no formal organization which can scrutinize corruption among MPs. The Counter Corruption Commission can only investigate permanent bureaucrats. The establishment of an ombudsman may help in this respect.

MPs and ministers should have to declare their assets upon taking and leaving office. The information should be available for the public to see. Periodic valuation of their assets will provide a useful check on their activities. Ways must be found to improve the efficiency of MPs in their task as representatives of the people. For example, offices for provincial MPs should be set up in each province to help facilitate their work for the people.

Conclusion

From our study we found that civil servants, military people, police officers and persons with relatively low education and income such as slum dwellers, manual workers and farmers, view politicians as more corrupt than bureaucrats. They believe that politicians have power over bureaucrats, and that most politicians enter politics in order to enrich themselves and their followers. However, people with higher income and education, namely businessmen, politicians, academicians, people in professional occupations, media men and NGO workers view bureaucrats as more corrupt than politicians. They argue that the bureaucratic system has much greater autonomy than politicians. Further, it is more difficult to investigate the corrupt practices of bureaucrats than those of politicians. Bureaucrats are also more numerous and have more opportunities to be corrupt.

The prevalence of corruption among bureaucrats is partly linked to the historical roots of the bureaucratic system. But it is sustained by the weaknesses and loopholes in the bureaucratic system, by negative social pressures, and by the conflict between the anachronisms of the bureaucratic system and the efficiency of modern business. Bureaucrats do not fully understand their role as public office holders.

The traditional practice of showing appreciation to officials and men in power by giving gifts or money (*sin nam jai*) overlaps with the modern conception of corruption. While there is nothing wrong with such a gift between two private individuals, it becomes corruption within the context of politics or bureaucracy. But many people do not make the distinction between the private realm and the official domain. This blurring of the boundaries makes many people accept the practice of presenting gifts and money to government officials as legitimate, as part of good Thai culture.

The bureaucratic structure is central to the corruption problem. The payment of low salaries tacitly encourages self-remuneration by moonlighting or the abuse of position for private gain. In many government departments, new recruits are forced to accept the established systems of syndicate corruption, and become inducted into a subculture of raising unofficial revenues and redistribution through the hierarchy of the department. Subordinates raise revenues to present to their superiors. Seniors raise revenues in order to distribute patronage to their subordinates. High-ranking officers create a wall to protect themselves and their subordinates from public scrutiny, often by citing the issue of national security. Recruitment and promotion based on patronage and nepotism converts some of these departments into the personal property of some groups of people, rather than true public offices.

The society also induces or condones corruption. The worship of wealth without any concern about its origins causes high-ranking officers to aspire to have high status based on wealth. Since they cannot get rich fast from their official salaries, they may take the short cut of abusing their powerful public position for private gain.

The increasing importance of modern business also promotes corruption. To overcome the slowness and inefficiency of bureaucratic systems, businessmen are prepared to pay since in the long run it may reduce their overall costs and increase their market advantages. This readiness to pay in turn induces bureaucrats to be slow and inefficient in order to extort payments.

The low moral standard of individual bureaucrats, and the tendency to live beyond their means, push some bureaucrats to engage in corruption. But most people think corruption is caused by weaknesses in the bureaucratic system rather than by the personal failures of individuals. These individual weaknesses should be countered by better systems of checks and balances.

Corruption among politicians also stems from faulty systems rather than from the low moral standards of individuals. Currently the political parties are dominated by merchants, big businessmen and influential people in provincial areas. Political parties seek political power by buying votes, and then use the political power they obtain to enrich themselves and their friends. They do not care about the problems of pollution, the deterioration of the natural environment, the widening gap between the rich and the poor, or social justice. Because of rampant corruption, national forests are destroyed, rivers and canals are polluted, factories, hotels, and department stores have collapsed. The readiness of ministers to accept gift cheques has helped to undermine the growth of public trust in democratic institutions.

Political parties must be reformed, and made independent of their business sponsors. Candidates for MPs must be scrutinized by the people before they can run in the general elections. By this means, many undesirable candidates can be screened out.

Combating bureaucratic corruption will require campaigns and actions at many different levels. It must entail legislation to improve bureaucratic systems and to institute better checks and balances. It will need popular campaigns to raise standards of personal, professional, and business ethics. Various institutions in society must play a part in these campaigns, including the family, educational bodies, and religious groups. The process of decision making within the public sector must be made more transparent. Representatives of the civil society must be allowed to participate in and scrutinize these decision-making process. Finally, freedom of the press and other media is crucial to ensure that people are well informed.

Any attempts to counter corruption among politicians must be done through strengthening of the civil society. In the end it is the people who will pressure the bureaucracy and the government to reform.

CONCLUSION

The rise of corruption *as an issue* in Thai politics in the late 1980s was not simply the result of an increase in the incidence of corruption. Indeed, the sums involved appear to have been small in comparison with the loot extracted by the military regimes from the 1950s to the 1970s. The rise of democratic institutions including parliament, press, and public opinion have closed down many of the simplest and most lucrative avenues of political corruption.

The rise of corruption as an issue was more a function of increasing competition for political power and revenues from corruption between the old power-holders in the military and civilian bureaucracy, and the new challengers in civilian politics, particularly those with a business background.

The prevalence of bureaucratic corruption stems from the systems of self-remuneration in the traditional bureaucracy. Officials were expected to remunerate themselves by taking a cut from revenues they collected, and extracting fees for services performed. In the transition to a modern *form* of bureaucracy, these practices were never erased. Meanwhile the systems for imposing moral and conventional limits on the *extent* of such self-remuneration have tended to decay.

In some sections of the bureaucracy there are corruption syndicates, which at the bottom collect fees for performance or non-performance of their duty, and which redistribute these sums right up to the top levels of the service. The practice of corruption has become embedded in the subculture of such government departments.

Corruption in the bureaucracy has helped to shape corruption in politics. Many of the provincial businessmen who came to dominate parliament and political parties in the 1980s owed their wealth and hence their political base to their ability to exploit the flexibility of the bureaucracy. They made huge profits by colluding with local officials to profit from government contracting, and to run semi-legal or criminal businesses. Then having bought votes to enter parliament, they continued to view politics as an extension of business, as an opportunity to make money.

Public opinion remains far from clear or coherent on the issue of what is corruption. The attitudes and vocabulary from the old traditional systems of official self-remuneration persist. Many forms of payment to officials are still rationalized as *sin nam jai*, the 'gifts of good will' from the public to people in power. The boundary between *sin nam jai* and bribery, extortion, corruption is not clearly marked.

The businessmen, officials, and politicians who are most involved in such transactions are more likely to condone them as gifts of good will. They also argue that the resulting flexibility and collusion actively promotes economic growth.

Two other social groups display a stricter attitude. Many middle class groups wish to impose a stricter concept of public office which would outlaw all forms of self-remuneration on principle. Many lower-echelon groups are growing increasingly aware that they are the ones who bear the cost of such systems of corruption. These two lobbies argue that the benefits in terms of economic growth are far outweighed by the social costs in terms of wasted resources, distorted distribution, environmental damage, and social inequity.

The control of corruption will require three strategies. First, the formal machinery for monitoring officials and politicians needs to be drastically improved. Most of the *means* to do this are already well-known and have been recommended by official commissions. What is lacking is the political *will* to implement them. Second, this *will* can only be generated by popular pressure. We cannot expect the bureaucrats and politicians who benefit from the political system to reform themselves. Thus it will be important to bring about changes in the political structure and moral environment to enable the people to exert greater pressure on those wielding power, through freedom of the press, decentralization of administrative power, greater transparency in government decision-making, and the reform of the political parties. Third, the public must be educated to exert moral and political pressure to outlaw corruption. The mobilization of such public pressure depends on a clearer understanding of the modern concepts of 'public office' and 'public service', and a more widespread awareness of the social costs and political risks which corruption entails. We hope this book has made some contribution to raising this awareness.

BIBLIOGRAPHY

Ammar Siamwalla (1992), 'Anand Government's Liberalisation: What For?', *Bangkok Post*, 12 March.

Anderson, Benedict (1990), 'Murder and Progress in Modern Siam', *New Left Review*, 181.

――― and Ruchira Mendiones (eds.) (1985), *In the Mirror*, Bangkok: DK Book House.

Anuman Rajadhon, Phraya (1972), *Kan suksa ruang prapheni khong thai lae chiwit chaothai samai korn* [The Study of Life and Customs of the Thai in the Past], Bangkok: Khlang Withaya Press.

Arlacchi, Pino (1988), *Mafia Business: the Mafia Ethic and the Spirit of Capitalism*, translated by Martin Ryle, Oxford University Press.

Battye, Noel Alfred (1974), 'The Military, Government and Society in Siam, 1868-1910', Ph.D. thesis, Cornell University.

Berg, Larry L. and others (eds) (1976), *Corruption in the American Political System*, Morristown, NJ: General Learning Press.

Bowring, Sir John (1969), *The Kingdom and People of Siam* With introduction by David K. Wyatt, Vol. 1, Kualalumpur: Oxford University Press.

Chanuan (1976), *Khabuan kan kong nai krom tamruat yuk or tor ror phon tamruat ek Prasert Ruchirawong* [Corruption Syndicates in the Police Department in the Time of Police Director General Prasert Ruchirawong], Bangkok.

Chartchai Na Chiangmai (1983), 'Parapolitical Behaviour of Northern Thai Villagers: An Application of Social Network Concepts', Ph.D. Thesis, University of Wisconsin.

Chubb, Judith (1982), *Patronage, Power and Poverty in Southern Italy: A Tale of Two Cities*, Cambridge University Press.

Coughlin, Richard, J. (1976), *Double Identity: the Chinese in Modern Thailand*, Westport, CT: Greenwood Press (Reprint of the 1960 publication by Hong Kong University Press).

Damri Chokset (1993), *'Kan kratham kwamphit khong kharatchakan tamruat: sahet lae matrakan nayobai pongkan'* [Misdeeds of the Policemen and Preventive Measures], M.A. thesis, Graduate School, Sathaban Technology Sangkhom.

Damrong Rachanuphap, Prince (1952), *Thesaphiban* [Local Administration], Bangkok: Khlang Withaya Press.

Eisenstadt, S.N. and Roniger, L. (1984), *Patrons, Clients and Friends. Interpersonal Relations and the Structure of Trust in Society*, Cambridge University Press.

Hanks, Lucien M. (1982), 'Merit and Power in the Thai Social Order', *American Anthropologist*, LXIV.

Huntington, Samuel P. (1968), 'Modernisation and Corruption', in *Political Order in Changing Societies*, New Haven, CT: Yale University Press.

Johnston, David Bruce (1980), 'Bandit, Nakleng, and Peasant in Rural Thai Society', *Contributions to Asian Studies*, XV.

Kanjanee Somkiatkul (1976), 'Corruption: An Analysis of the Modernisation During the Reign of King Rama V (1868-1910)', M.A. Thesis, Department of History, Graduate School, Chulalongkorn University.

McCoy, Alfred W. (1991), *The Politics of Heroin: CIA Complicity in Drug Trade*, Lawrence Hill Books.

McCoy, Alfred W. (1972), *The Politics of Heroin in Southeast Asia*, NY, Harper & Row Publishers.

Morell, D. (1975), 'Legislatures and Political Development: The Problem of Corruption', paper read at the Conference on Legislatures in Contemporary Societies, Albany, NY, January.

Myrdal, Gunnar (1968), *Asian Drama: An Enquiry into the Poverty of Nations*, 3 Vols, New York: Twentieth Century Fund.

Naruemon Nitayajin (1989), *'Jao mu huey taidin: suksa chapho korani itthiphon thang kanmuang'* [Illegal Lottery Financiers: a Study of Those with Political Influence], M.A. thesis, Graduate School, Chulalongkorn University.

Neher, Clark D. (1977), 'Political Corruption in a Thai Province', *Journal of Developing Areas*, 7:4.

Neher, Clark D. (1988), *'Khorrapchan thang kanmuang nai tang jangwat prathet thai'* [Corruption in a Thai Province], in Chai-Anan Samudavanija, James C. Scott (eds.) translated by Sitthiphan Phutthahun, *Khorrapchan* [Corruption], Bangkok: Kopfai.

Nucharin Kasemsukworarat (1990), 'The Economic Analysis of Hired Motorcycle Service in Bangkok', M.Econ. (English Language Programme), Faculty of Economics, Thammasat University.

Ockey, James, (1992), 'Business Leaders, Gangsters and the Middle Class: societal groups and civilian rule', Ph.D. Thesis, Cornell University.

———. (1993), 'Capital Accumulation by Other Means: Provincial Crime, Corruption, and the Bureaucratic Polity', paper presented at the 5th International Conference on Thai Studies, SOAS, London.

Office of Auditor General (OAG) (1982, 1983, 1985, 1986, 1987, 1988, 1989, 1990), *Annual Report*, Bangkok.

Office of the Prime Minister (1977), *Phaendin Thai* [The Kingdom of Thailand], Vol. 1, Bangkok.

Owens, Cynthia (1992), 'Thai Military's Financial Power Remains', *Asian Wall Street Journal*, 16 June.

Pasuk Phongpaichit (1992), 'The Politics of Economic Policy Reform in Thailand', in *The Politics of Economic Reform in Southeast Asia*, edited by David G. Timberman, Manila: The Asian Institute of Management.

Phongsan Khongtrikaew (1986), *'Krabuankan plianplaeng thang khaniyom lae thasana khati khong nai tamruat chan sanyabat'* [The process of value change and attitudes of police officers], M.A. thesis, Graduate School, Chulalongkorn University.

Phim Thai (1967), *Khadi rathamontri 'gin pha'* [The Case of a Minister Eating the Forest], Bangkok.

Preecha Sa-artson (1992), *'Banchidam lang jao pho ngan thagun tamruat thai'* [Blacklisting of Jao Pho: a Challenge to the Thai Police], *Krungthep Thurakit*, July.

Purachai Piamsombun (1983), *'Itthiphon phon prayot lae pruthikam nai ongkan tamruat thai'* [Influence, interests and behaviour in the Thai police organization], *Warasan phatthana borihan sat* [Public Administration Journal], I:23.

———. (1979), 'The Economics of Corruption', *The Journal of Public Economics*, 4.

Riggs, Fred W. (1966), *Thailand: The Modernisation of a Bureaucratic Polity*, Honolulu, HI: East-West Center Press.

Sannathi Prayunrat (1989), *'Panha khong kan patirup krom tamruat'* [Problems of the Reform of the Police Department], M.A. thesis, Graduate School, Chulalongkorn University.

Scott, James C. (1972), *Comparative Political Corruption*, Englewood Cliffs, NJ: Prentice-Hall.

Skinner, G. W. (1957), *Chinese Society in Thailand: An Analytical History*, Ithaca, NY: Cornell University Press.

Sombat Chantornvong (1992), 'The Roles of Local Godfathers in Thai Economy and Polity', in Pasuk Phongpaichit, Sungsidh Piriyarangsan (eds.), *Rat, thun, jao pho thongthin lae sangkhom thai* [State, Capital, Local Godfathers and Thai

Society], The Political Economy Centre, Faculty of Economics, Chulalongkorn University.

Somkiat Wantana (1993), *'Nak thurakit thongthin kap prachathippatai thai'* [Provincial Businessmen and Democracy in Thailand], in *Chon chan khlang bon krasae prachathippatai thai* [The Middle Class and Thai Democracy], The Political Economy Centre, Faculty of Economics, Chulalongkorn University.

Somrudee Nicrowattanayingyong (1991), 'Development Planning, Politics and Paradox: A Study of Khon Kaen, A Regional City in Northeastern Thailand', Ph.D. thesis, Syracuse University.

Sondhi Limthongkul (1991), *'Jao pho mai mi wan tai'* [Jao Pho Never Die], *Phujatkan Sutsapda,* 15-21 April.

Sungsidh Piriyarangsan (1983), *Thai Bureaucratic Capitalism (1932-1960)*, Bangkok: Chulalongkorn University Social Science Research Institute.

Suriyan Sakthaisong (1990), *Senthang Mafia* [The Path of the Mafia], Bangkok: Matichon Publishing.

Suwit Paitayawat (1978), 'The Evolution of the Rural Economy in Central Region, Thailand', M.A. Thesis, Faculty of Arts, Chulalongkorn University.

Tamada, Yoshifumi (1991), 'Itthiphon and Amnat: an Informal Aspect of Thai Politics', *Southeast Asian Studies,* 29:4.

Thak Chaloemtiarana (1979), *Thailand: The Politics of Despotic Paternalism*, Bangkok: Social Science Association of Thailand, Thai Khadi Institute, Thammasat University.

Thinapan Nakata (1977), *'Kan khorrapchan nai wong ratchakan thai: kan samruet khwam kit hen khong kharatchakan lae prachachon'* [Corruption in Thai Public Administration: A Survey of Opinions among the Public Servants and the People], *Warasan phatthana borihan sat* [Journal of Public Administration] 17, July.

Teeranat Karnjana-uksorn (1993), *'Thahan kap thurakit'* [The Military and Business], in Sungsidh Piriyarangsan and Pasuk Phongpaichit (eds.), *Chon chan khlang bon krasae prachathipatai thai* [The Middle Class and Thai Democracy], Bangkok: The Political Economy Centre, Faculty of Economics, Chulalongkorn University.

Turton, Andrew (1989), 'Local Powers and Rural Differentiation', in Gillian Hart, Andrew Turton and Benjamin White (eds.), *Agrarian Transformations in South-east Asia: The State and Local Processes of Accumulation*, Berkeley, Los Angeles, Oxford: University of California Press.

Ukrist Pathamanan (1983), *'Saharat amerika kap nayobai setthakit thai 2503-2513'* [The US and Thai Economic Policy 1960-1970], M.A. Thesis, Department of International Relations, Graduate School, Chulalongkorn University.

Van Roy, Edward (1970), 'On the Theory of Corruption', *Economic Development and Cultural Change*, 19:1.

Viengrat Naetipoh (1989), 'Semi-Businessman Semi-Gangster', *Jotmai khao sangkomsat*, The Social Science Association of Thailand, August-October.

Viwanna Theva-alangkul (1984), '*Nayobai khong rathaban kap tamruat phuthorn 2440-2465*' [Government Policy and the Gendarmerie, 1897-1922], M.A. thesis, Silpakorn University.

Woradet Chansorn (1983), '*Kan patirup tamruat thai*' [The Reform of the Thai Police], *Warasan phatthana borihan sat* [Public Administration Journal], 4:23, October.

INDEX

51, 155-6, 159-63, 174-8, 180-7;
and military, 10-11, 14, 16-18, 47-
50, 143-5, 147-8;
and politics, 12-18, 39-47, 151-5,
157-61, 164-5, 175-8, 183-7;
as an issue, 1-2, 6-10, 21-2, 187;
definitions, 2-6, 19-21, 133-5, 166-
74
Counter Corruption Commission
(CCC), 9, 29-37, 46, 53-4, 179-81,
183
coup, 1991, 2, 14, 16-17, 44, 154
Customs Department, 155

Damrong Rachanuphap, Krom
Phraya, 110, 114, 117
Damrong Singtothong (Hia Sui), 68,
70
De Tocqueville, Alexis, 19
democracy, 2, 14-18, 22, 155-61
Democrat Party, 75, 79, 95, 101, 103,
157
drugs, see narcotics

East Asiatic Company, 80, 114
eastern seaboard, 62-3, 67
Ekaparp (Solidarity) party, 65, 81,
96, 157
elections, 15-16, 18, 69, 72, 83, 93-5,
103, 153-4
Electricity Generating Authority
(EGAT), 43, 44
energy organization, 34
Express Transit Organization, 35

Fishery Department, 36
Forestry Department, 36, 43

gambling, 71, 74-5, 82, 87, 122, 128
gin muang, 7, 110-11, 115
gunmen, 61, 65, 69, 72, 74, 76, 82, 87,
96

Hanks, Lucien, 3, 4
Highway Department, 35
hua kanaen (vote bank), 64, 68, 83, 94,
99
Huntington, Samuel, 19-21

India, v-vi
Internal Security Operations
Command (ISOC), 63
Irrigation Department, 34, 36, 37
Isan Khiew (green northeast) project,
75, 92

jao pho, 12-13, 17, 56-107, 178
Japan, ix, 22
Jongchai Tiengtham, 94
Jumpol Sukparangsi (Sia Jiew), 63-5,
102

kamnan, see village heads
Kamnan Bo, see Somchai Kunpluem
Kamol Thongthammachat, 78
Khon Kaen, 73-6, 96
Khuang Aphaiwong, 5
Kiang Jungprasert (Long Ju Kiang),
63, 102
Kitsangkom (Social Action Party),
65, 67, 69-70, 76, 93, 95-6, 156-7
Klaeo Thanikul, 75
Korea, South, ix, v-vi
Kriangsak Chomanan, General, 78
Kukrit Pramoj, 65, 95
Kwamwangmai (New Aspiration)
party, 92, 96, 156-7

Laem Chabang, see eastern seaboard
Land Department, 28, 32, 36, 155
Lavalin company, 45
local government, 88-90
logging, see timber business
Lottery Bureau, 26, 52
lottery, underground, 63, 74, 87, 123,
130